Sun Tzu's

THE
ART
OF
WAR

Plus

The
Art
of
Marketing

Strategy for Conquering Markets

Gary Gagliardi

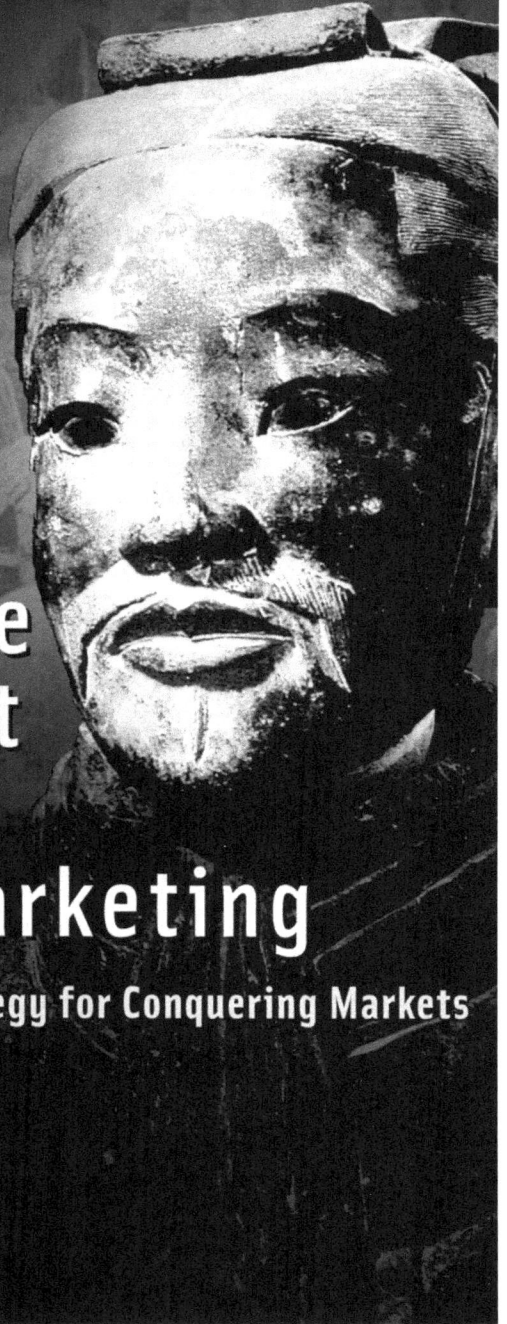

"...a must read for every marketing executive."

"The Art of War Plus The Art of Marketing from Clearbridge Publishing, is a must read for every marketing executive. Gary Gagliardi creatively interprets Sun Tzu's classic text into straightforward winning advice for conducting marketing campaigns. In addition, the side-by-side presentation of both texts allows readers to compare Sun Tzu's words with Mr. Gagliardi's marketing interpretations. This book is guaranteed to provide you with the motivation to capture your markets!"

DR. D. STEVEN WHITE, Ph.D., Dept. of Marketing & Business Information Systems, Charlton College of Business, University of Massachusetts-Dartmouth

The Art of War Plus
The Art of Marketing

Business
Ben Franklin
Book Award
2004 - Finalist

This book contains the only award-winning translation of Sun Tzu's *The Art of War*

Award Recognition for *Art of War* Strategy Books
by Gary Gagliardi

The Golden Key to Strategy

Psychology/Self-Help
Ben Franklin
Book Award
2006 - Winner

*The Art of War Plus
The Ancient Chinese Revealed*

Multicultural Nonfiction
Independent Publishers
Book Award
2003 - Winner

*Making Money by Speaking:
The Spokesperson Strategy*

Career
Foreword Magazine
Book of the Year
2007 - Finalist

Strategy for Sales Managers

Business
Independent Publishers
Book Award
2006 - Semi-Finalist

*The Warrior Class:
306 Lessons in Strategy*

Self-Help
Foreword Magazine
Book of the Year
2005 - Finalist

Strategy Against Terror

Philosophy
Foreword Magazine
Book of the Year
2005 - Finalist

*The Ancient Bing-fa:
Martial Arts Strategy*

Sports
Foreword Magazine
Book of the Year
2007 - Finalist

*The Art of War
Plus Its Amazing Secrets*

Multicultural Nonfiction
Independent Publishers
Book Award
2005 - Finalist

The Warrior's Apprentice

Youth Nonfiction
Independent Publishers
Book Award
2006 - Semi-Finalist

Sun Tzu's

THE
ART
OF
WAR

Plus

The Art of Marketing
Strategy for Conquering Markets

by Gary Gagliardi

Science of Strategy Institute

Clearbridge Publishing

Published by
Science of Strategy Institute, Clearbridge Publishing
 suntzus.com   scienceofstrategy.org

Fourth Edition
Also sold as *The Art of War for Marketing Warriors*
Copyright 1999, 2001, 2003, 2013, 2014 Gary Gagliardi
ISBN 978-1-929194-74-2 (13-digit) 1-929194-74-9 (10-digit)

Clearbridge Publishing and its logo, a transparent bridge, are the trademarks of Clearbridge Publishing.

Manufactured in the United States of America.
Interior and cover graphic design by Dana and Jeff Wincapaw.
Original Chinese calligraphy by Tsai Yung, Green Dragon Arts, www.greendragonarts.com.

Publisher's Cataloging-in-Publication Data
Sun-tzu, 6th cent. B.C.
Political science
     [Sun-tzu ping fa, English]
     The art of war plus the art of politics / Sun Tzu and Gary Gagliardi.
     p. 226 cm. 23
     Includes introduction to basic competitive philosophy of Sun Tzu
ISBN 978-1-929194-74-2 (13-digit) 1-929194-74-9 (10-digit)

Clearbridge Publishing's books may be purchased for business, for any promotional use, or for special sales. Please contact:

Clearbridge Publishing
PO Box 33772, Seattle, WA 98133
Phone: (206)542-8947 Fax: (206)546-9756

Contents

**The Art of War Plus
The Art of Marketing**

Foreword

Sun Tzu for Marketing

The purpose of this book is to introduce those in marketing campaigns to the strategic principles of Sun Tzu's *The Art of War* and their use in communicating with potential customers. Sun Tzu's strategy consists of more than two hundred general principles. Each principle can be applied to any competitive arena in a systematic way. We call these principles *Sun Tzu's Warrior's Playbook*. This work is meant simply as a basic orientation to this method of competitive thinking. Unlike other books on strategy, this work is not a work about strategic planning. It is a work teaching strategic agility, "strategility" for short, the ability to adapt instantly to changes in the competitive environment. In it we use Sun Tzu's original text as a line-by-line template for applying those principles to working in the various aspects of marketing.

Marketing Strategy

How does *The Art of War* apply to marketing? The Chinese title of this work, *Bing-fa*, means literally "martial arts," but Sun Tzu uses the term more broadly to mean "competitive skills." Unlike other works on military strategy, Sun Tzu designed his book to explain the secrets of competition in the broadest terms possible. The only differences between competition in the business arena and military warfare are the types of tools used and the nature of the battleground. The only weapon that this book teaches you to use is the most powerful competitive weapon of all—the human mind.

To borrow from the German general Carl von Clausewitz, marketing is war by other means. In many ways, today's competing businesses in the marketplace resemble the contesting city-states of Sun Tzu's era—in scale and psychology—much more than today's nation-states do.

In Sun Tzu's view, success goes not to the most aggressive but to those who best understand their situation and what their alternatives really are. When you have mastered Sun Tzu's system of strategy, you will be able to almost instantly analyze marketing situations, spot market opportunities, and make the appropriate decisions.

In our adaptation for marketing, the rules of strategy agility are tailored to help you in your role as an organizer, communicator, and persuader. This book addresses a range of challenges, including evaluating your potential prospects and customers, planning a marketing campaign, adjusting to specific market condition, diagnosing customer behavior, and so on. As a market campaigner, you have to face a wide variety of issues, and we try to address a broad spectrum of them in this book.

In this work, we present each stanza of *The Art of War* on the left-hand pages, side by side with an adaptation of that stanza to the challenges of marketing on the right-hand pages. This adaption converts Sun Tzu's ideas from the military arena into the world of marketing as consistently as possible. We start by defining marketing as a contest, or, more precisely, a comparison, for the customers' spending dollar.

Sun Tzu's underlying competitive principles are rich and complex. At our website, SunTzus.com , we explore these principles and their step-by-step application in great detail. As an introduction, this book is more limited. We explore the general relationships among these principles in the Introduction, which follows.

The Art of War Plus The Art of Marketings is a different type of book on market positioning. It addresses decision-making strategy in its most critical form. It won't give you any tricks for composing ads or clever phrases for campaign slogans. There are plenty of books that address those techniques. Instead, this book focuses on the core issues of market strategic positioning. It teaches the kind of thinking, planning, and decision-making that it takes for a person to have a successful career in marketing.

The book first addresses large-scale issues in marketing that other books usually overlook. You cannot be successful in marketing unless you are marketing the right products in the right marketplaces for the right reason. As you progress deeper into the book, the text delves into a variety of more specific situations and special conditions that will help you with the specific marketing campaigns that you might be engaged in.

Competition as Positioning

Why is Sun Tzu's strategy so powerful? Sun Tzu saw that our competitive instincts are all wrong. People think of competition as a threat or a fight. When people are challenged, they react in one of two ways. Sometimes, they run away. Other times, people attack those who threaten them. Psychologists call this the "flight or fight reflex." Sun Tzu taches that seeing competition in terms of threats is foolish.

Sun Tzu teaches that competition is simply a comparison. Competition is unavoidable because everyone is constantly comparing everything. People must compare in order to make choices. This comparison is the basis of all market positioning.

The true opposite of competition is the absence of choice. If we had no choices, we would have nothing to compare. Competition wouldn't exist. Marketplaces wouldn't exist without a choice among different products and sales channels. We must understand how buying comparisons affects the choices of our potential products, customers, and marketing niches.

In developing our marketing version, we were as consistent as possible in translating the ideas from the military arena to the marketplace. We simply define marketing as a battle for the customer's mind. The military generals addressed by Sun Tzu become today's business owners and marketing managers. The nation for whom the army fights becomes the company that marketing managers are trying to promote. The contested terrain translates into a segment of the marketplace.

Positions in Dynamic Situations

People misunderstand the true nature of success. Success doesn't come from using size, power, or money. It comes from using elements of your position to advance your position, winning the most profitable market share, usually measure in sales.

People think they can win the battle of competitive comparison by tearing down opposing products. They fight for position through wars of attrition. This is costly to everyone involved. Instead of fighting, Sun Tzu teaches you how to advance your position so that people cannot fight you—and ideally, over time, want to join you.

In Sun Tzu's view, the secret to warfare is not just winning battles. It is winning them quickly and economically. Victory alone is not enough. Sun Tzu teaches that true success is "making victory pay," that is, making victory profitable and rewarding. You must be wary of costly "victories" that consume your time and energy but fail to bring you long-term success in winning a campaign.

This economic view maps extremely well onto any serious approach to marketing. Our goal in marketing is not just to win market awareness, market share, or even customers; rather, it is to do so in a way that profits the organization. Anyone can spend money on advertising and promotion. Anyone can sell products at a loss. The real challenge is leveraging the costs of marketing into profits for the company.

Though *bing-fa* shows you how to find success in competitive situations, Sun Tzu's recipe for success is to avoid unnecessary conflict, that is, trying to destroy the positions of others. He sees such conflict as inherently costly. Again, this closely matches the goals in marketing warfare. You must convince potential customers that your product, service, or company is their very best choice without conflicting with their existing assumptions about the marketplace, especially concerning their past choices. Instead, you must show them what has changed to make a different choice in the future.

When we adapt Sun Tzu's methods of warfare to marketing, the lessons that emerge are intriguing.

First, Sun Tzu teaches that winning a market is not enough. The goal is to win easily, with minimal costs. The first step in making a profit is limiting cost. Since marketing is expensive, the goal is to win customers quickly and efficiently. The essential ingredient in winning easily is picking the right battles. Sun Tzu gives us a formula for reasoning out our plan for victory. We want to fight for markets only in situations where we are certain to win, and we want to be certain that winning is well worth the cost.

Next, his lessons are extremely specific about what to do in certain situations. He wants us to pay close attention to the details of our competitive circumstances. He enumerates different field conditions, different types of opponents, different leadership mistakes, different competitive signals, and so on. Although Sun Tzu wrote about warfare, when translated to marketing, these detailed lists are still surprisingly complete. Their advice is useful to anyone analyzing a market situation.

Next, Sun Tzu offers his "cooperative" view of competition. In his eye, we cannot win through our own actions. We don't create successful markets. We can defend our existing markets from loss, but we discover new opportunities only when market forces create them. The secret to success is recognizing a good market when it presents itself. This may seem like a patient approach, but Sun Tzu thought that opportunities were abundant. Every problem creates an opportunity. We just fail to see it.

The secret is what we call strategility, recognizing these opportunities when they present themselves and instantly having the confidence to act on them. Customer will buy—or not buy—as they have bought before unless something changes in the environment to get them to rethink their purchases. Because you must leverage change, marketing often requires watchful patience. At other times, marketing requires instant reaction. Sun Tzu argues that opportunities are always abundant, since every problem creates an opportunity. The problem is that opportunities are easily overlooked, difficult to recognize and act upon.

Finally, Sun Tzu's view of competition is knowledge-intensive. He sees victory going to the person who is the most knowledgeable. And he recognizes creativity as a special and important type of knowledge. In Sun Tzu, there is no substitute for good information. *The Art of War's* last chapter, USING SPIES, makes it clear how essential good information is. In the marketing adaptation, this chapter becomes USING MARKET RESEARCH. These chapters make it clear that Sun Tzu understood the value of information in the economy. He clearly saves his most important message for last. He says outright that nothing is as important as acquiring good information.

The universal utility of Sun Tzu's principles means that you can apply them in different ways in different situations. With more study, you will develop more insight into Sun Tzu's methods and your own situation.

As your situation changes, different parts of the book will become more important. In general, the book is organized so that the broadest and longest-term issues, such as strategic analysis, are addressed in the initial chapters. Later chapters tend to focus on the special challenges encountered under specific conditions.

Later chapters tend to focus on the special challenges encountered under specific conditions of a marketing campaign. Do not expect to appreciate all of Sun Tzu's principles in one reading. Time spent studying Sun Tzu's system of strategility is always time well invested.

Reading this book is simply the first step in mastering the warrior's world of competitive philosophy. As I have said, Sun Tzu's strategic system is sophisticated and deep. Much of its sophistication is not readily apparent simply from reading the text. The Science of Strategy Institute has spent more than a decade detailing the use of Sun Tzu's principles in modern competition. This marketing adaptation helps you start using Sun Tzu's ideas, but if you are interested in mastering this powerful competitive strategy in business generally and marketing specifically, it only scratches the surface of what is hidden in the work.

If you want to continue your study of Sun Tzu's principles, please visit SunTzus.com. Every day on that site, we explain one of Sun Tzu's general principles in detail. Those who become paid members of the Institute get on-line access to our complete *Sun Tzu's Art of War Playbook*, which explains hundreds of Sun Tzu's principles in terms of simple step-by-step rules. The Institute also offers a number of audio books, seminars, and—most importantly—on-line training courses to make Sun Tzu's methods instinctive.

When we started codifying Sun Tzu's strategic rules, we didn't realize how big the task was. In the end, the work encompassed over two hundred and thirty articles. Each article explains one strategic principle and its relationships to interconnected principles. Developed as a framework for a complete course of strategic studies, these articles break down each general principle into a series of steps or components that are illustrated by examples from modern competition. These articles have been organized into nine areas of strategic skill. These articles now are also available in nine volumes, each focusing on a single strategic skill area, both as ebooks and as printed books.

Why is this work on developing Sun Tzu's ideas into rules necessary? As you will see in reading this work, Sun Tzu's *The Art of War* is not a "training book" in the modern Western sense. It is a list of formulas written the context of the scientific philosophy of the era. Adapting these ideas into the terms of modern marketing is a start, but understanding all these concepts is nearly impossible for modern readers without examples or exercises. Like Euclid's Geometry, simply reading the work gives us few useful tools. Our development of the *Playbook* and our training exercises was necessary to help people practice in these methods in their everyday life.

✦ ✦ ✦

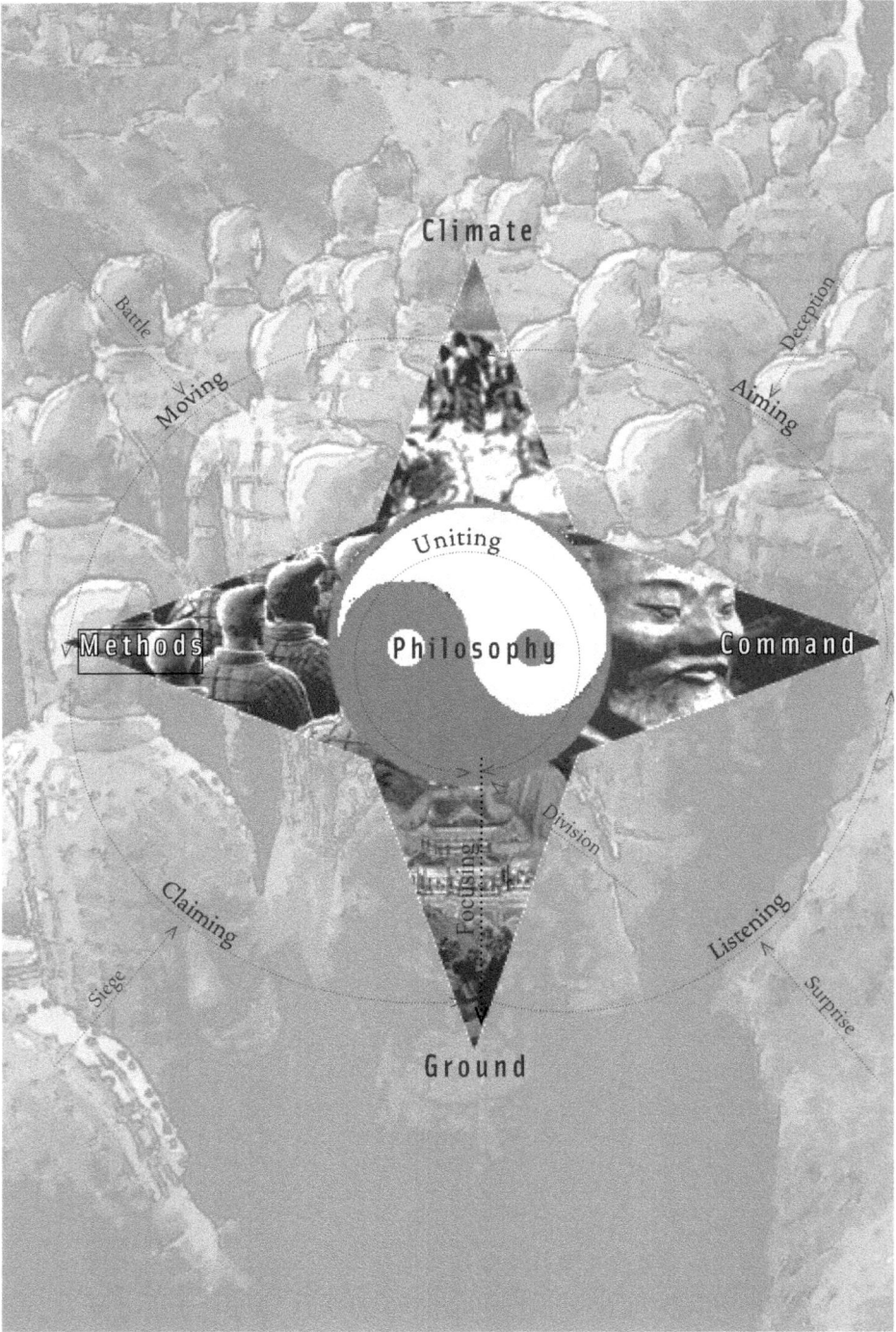

Climate

Deception

Battle

Moving

Aiming

Uniting

Methods

Philosophy

Command

Focusing

Division

Claiming

Listening

Siege

Surprise

Ground

Introduction:

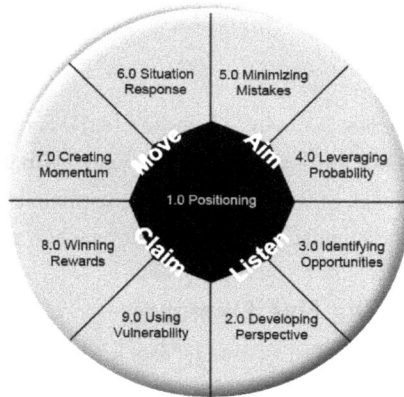

6.0 Situation Response
5.0 Minimizing Mistakes
7.0 Creating Momentum
4.0 Leveraging Probability
Move
Aim
1.0 Positioning
8.0 Winning Rewards
Claim
Listen
3.0 Identifying Opportunities
9.0 Using Vulnerability
2.0 Developing Perspective

Sun Tzu's Basic Concepts

This book teaches the use of classical strategy to achieve success in marketing. To put you on the path of the marketing strategist, what we call the "marketing warrior," let us clarify the elements of Sun Tzu's strategic system. If you are new to Sun Tzu's strategic principles, you will find *The Art of War* and our marketing adaptation, *The Art of Marketing*, much easier to understand if you first familiarize yourself with a few basic concepts, metaphors, and analogies. As with all traditional Chinese science, this system is based on five elements and the nine skills. This introduction gives you an overview of these elements of his strategic system.

As defined by Sun Tzu, strategy is not a system of planning. Planning, in the sense of prioritizing a list of activities, works in controlled environments where you can know how others will respond to your decisions. Strategy works in competitive environments where your decisions collide with the decisions of others, creating conditions that no one planned. In competitive environments, your success depends on predicting how others will respond.

Sun Tzu taught that in these competitive environments, success is not a matter of winning fights with other people. Instead success depends on building and advancing strategic positions. The idea is to create positions that others cannot attack and that ideally they want to join. Sun Tzu teaches that a general who fights a hundred battles and wins a hundred battles is not a good general. A good general is one who finds a way to win without fighting a single battle. Strategy teaches that you win by building the right positions and advancing those positions while avoiding conflict.

The Five Elements

Sun Tzu's strategic tool kit is based on the *five element system* introduced in the first section of his first chapter. These five elements—philosophy, heaven, ground, the leader, and methods—define a strategic position and provide the backbone of strategic analysis. All the other components of his system—deception, unity, knowledge, and so on—have very specific and logical relationships to these five elements. The depth and sophistication of the system require some explanation.

Sun Tzu taught that every competitive situation depends upon the unique position of a given competitor within the larger competitive environment. Understanding positions is the first skill that his strategic system teaches. Strategy is focused on building up or advancing your position in such a way that opponents cannot attack you and ideally others want to join you. In choosing between your product and a competitor's, the customer decides based upon your relative positions within this larger competitive environment. All the other skills of his toolkit for advancing positions—developing perspective, identifying opportunities, and so on (see the first diagram in this introduction)—develop better positions from these elements.

The focus on the competitive environment was a unique feature of Sun Tzu's work, at least until Darwin. As with so many of Sun Tzu's basic concepts, he describes the environment as two opposite and yet complementary halves, *heaven (climate)* and *ground (earth)*. Heaven and ground are the arenas of time and place within which you compete for your customers' dollars.

Heaven represents the uncontrollable passage of time, but more accurately it describes change. It is often translated as "climate" or "weather" in the text. It is best to think of heaven as trends that change over time. The cycle of the seasons is the most obvious trend in the natural environment, but every organization has its own business cycle and market climate. People's attitudes and emotions are also an important part of Sun Tzu's concept of climate. In the marketing professional's environment, industry trends, buying cycles, product fashions, and distribution process changes all affect marketing. Each change is an opportunity to change people's minds about your product. These business cycles cannot be controlled but they can be recognized and, to some degree, predicted.

Ground is the economic foundation on which your strategic position is based. It is both where you fight and what you fight for. As a marketing person, you can think of the ground as your markets, your competitors, and your potential customers. Unlike heaven, which is largely beyond your control, the most important aspect of the ground is that its changes result only from your choices and actions. You choose your customers. You choose what to say about your products and company. Choosing positions, moving to them, and utilizing them are the basis of Sun Tzu's strategic methods.

The first two components of your strategic position define the external time and place of your strategic position.

You and your company are positioned within a *heaven* of changing market trends. Your product can be ahead of these trends or behind them. All products represent a prediction about what is important for the future. Your customers are making decisions today about what will be important in the future. All the emotions involved in the marketing cycle are based upon the fears and uncertainties about what the future will bring.

Your strategic position is grounded on the world (*earth*) of real customers. These customers are your base of financial support. You battle with competitors for the limited amount of money these customers are willing to spend. Correctly analyzing this ground and picking the right customers is the basis of your success.

Within the larger competitive environment, the unique characteristics of both you and your organization are also part of your strategic positions. Sun Tzu breaks the important characteristics of a competitor into two opposite and complementary components: the *leader* and *methods*.

A *leader* is a person who makes the decisions in a contest. Marketing people are leaders because they must make marketing choices. All customers are also leaders, that is, decision-makers because they choose what to buy. Leadership is the realm of individual character. A leader masters the strategy so that he or she can make the right decisions quickly.

Methods are the techniques of organization. Success depends upon working with other people. Methods are the realm where you interact with other people. Marketing people make decisions as individuals, but you must work with product development, your sales team, and your channel partners. You must also connect to your target customers and the way they buy. The job of the marketing person is to connect the methods of his or her organization in making sales to the methods of customers in making purchases.

Binding and underlying your strategic position is its *philosophy*. *Philosophy* is the unique values that provide the core of a strategic position. In business, we call this a company mission or purpose. Philosophy is a shared goal. A core philosophy provides marketing people and their companies with unity and focus. Your philosophy also unites you with your customers.

Listen Aim Move Claim

Once you see your strategic position clearly in terms of these five factors, you advance your position. The balance of the book addresses specific methods a marketing person can use for advancing a position. However, all this information can be boiled down into four simple steps. Sun Tzu's terms for these four processes are *knowing, foreseeing, moving*, and *positioning*. More generally, we describe these steps are *listening for knowledge, aiming at opportunities, moving to openings*, and *claiming a position*. Every advance requires all four steps. If you miss a step, the process is more likely to create problems than to solve them.

Knowledge comes from understanding your ground, which requires *listening. Aim* means seeing how changing trends create an *opportunity* to advance. *Moving* means the ability to change methods to take advantage of an *opening*. *Claiming* means reaping the rewards from a new ground *position*.

These four steps can be further broken down into a list of eight skills. Remember, Sun Tzu's first skill is understanding positions. Listening requires Sun Tzu's second key strategic skill of an outside developing perspective on your position and his third strategic skill of using change for identifying opportunities. Aiming requires Sun Tzu's fourth and fifth skills, leveraging probability and minimizing mistakes. Moving requires his six and seventh skills of situation response and creating momentum. Claiming requires his eighth and ninth skills of winning rewards and understanding vulnerabilities. All of these skills are covered in detail in our *Sun Tzu's Playbook*, referenced at the end of each chapter.

Each of these four steps leads naturally to the next in an endless cycle of advances. In marketing, they form a spiral, working from the general market to your specific customers. Each sale improves your position in the next cycle. The more you learn about your ground, the more you need to identify new opportunities. Aiming at a new opportunity necessitates moving to new methods. Moving must give you a new position that you can claim. Claiming new ground creates new opportunities to listen and learn. Even if your attempted advance fails to yield profitable new ground, it cannot fail to generate new knowledge, which is the basis of your next cycle and your inevitable success as a marketing warrior.

Consciously or unconsciously, you go through this cycle every time you advance your position. When a decision is unsuccessful, it is simply because one of these four steps was not properly executed.

The Art of War is a complete guide to executing these four steps in a wide variety of situations. However, much of it is written in a kind of code. These four steps are usually referenced in terms metaphors. Listening for knowledge is referenced as sound. Thunder, music, and drums are all metaphors for listening. Aim is described as vision. Colors, lightning, and so on are all metaphors for foresight. Moving is marching. Claiming a position is variously described as gathering food, building, eating, digging in, and so on. We make all of these ideas easier to understand by adapting these metaphors into more easily understood management terms.

Just as these four steps are defined in terms of the five factors of a position, other strategic responses are defined in terms of these four steps. *Surprise* undermines knowledge. *Deception* confuses aim. *Battle*—which means meeting a challenge, not necessarily conflict—counters movement. *Siege* tries to overturn a position.

For a picture of Sun Tzu's system of five elements, four steps, and four responses, you can refer to the diagram that precedes this introduction. ♦ ♦ ♦

Heaven

Methods   Leader

Philosophy

Ground

Chapter 1

計

Analysis — Research

All marketing strategy starts with understanding the existing market and your position in it. Based directly on the science of strategy, *The Art of Marketing* adaptation of Sun Tzu offers a very specific system for analysis and market research. This system pares marketing research down to its bare essentials. It teaches that only a handful of factors are ultimately important in understanding your market position, but that analyzing those factors requires discipline.

Five key components define your strategic position in the marketplace. Only these key elements determine where and how your position can be advanced. To use strategy effectively, you must compare your position directly with those of your real competitors. Strategy teaches that all positions are relative. Your market position is defined by the position of your existing competition.

This market analysis must be based on fact, not emotion. You must gather information from outsiders. As you evaluate information, you cannot take anything at face value. In markets, people are consciously trying to control other people's perceptions. Plus, people are constantly fooling themselves about their true market position. Since everyone is constantly looking for openings, you need to practice deception when you position yourself, misleading your competitors as much as possible.

Strategic analysis is a search for the measurable in marketing. You must continually balance the positive and negative aspects of whatever you can measure.

The Art of War: **Analysis**

SUN TZU SAID:

This is war. 1
It is the most important skill in the nation.
It is the basis of life and death.
It is the philosophy of survival or destruction.
You must know it well.

6Your skill comes from five factors.
Study these factors when you plan war.
You must insist on knowing your situation.
1.   Discuss philosophy.
2.   Discuss the climate.
3.   Discuss the ground.
4.   Discuss leadership.
5.   Discuss military methods.

14Start with your military philosophy.
Command your people in a way that gives them a
higher shared purpose.
You can lead them to death.
You can lead them to life.
They must never fear danger or dishonesty.

STRATEGY:

Winning is the skill of leveraging positions. Analyze your position by looking at five simple factors.

The Art of Marketing: **Research**

A MARKETING WARRIOR HEARS:

1 This is market competition.
Without marketing strategy, your organization will fail.
Marketing is the foundation of fortunes and failures.
Your marketing strategy is to preserve the best and destroy the rest.
You must see all aspects of your market position.

There are five aspects that define your position in a marketplace.
Weigh these factors in your market analysis.
You must insist on knowing your marketing situation.

1. Discuss your business mission.
2. Discuss the marketplace trends.
3. Discuss your market segment.
4. Discuss decision-making.
5. Discuss the marketing process.

MISSION:

Mission is the core of your market position. A clear mission creates strength and focus in your position.

Market positions begin with a business mission.
The true mission is an ideal goal that unites an organization with its customers.
This mission meets a challenge or need.
It must make a real difference in people's lives.
This true mission creates a bond of trust.

POSITION:

*Your position
exists within
a larger com-
petitive environ-
ment, which you
do not control.*

[19]Next, you have the climate.
It can be sunny or overcast.
It can be hot or cold.
It includes the timing of the seasons.

[23]Next is the terrain.
It can be distant or near.
It can be difficult or easy.
It can be open or narrow.
It also determines your life or death.

[28]Next is the commander.
He must be smart, trustworthy, caring, brave, and strict.

[30]Finally, you have your military methods.
They include the shape of your organization.
This comes from your management philosophy.
You must master their use.

[34]All five of these factors are critical.
As a commander, you must pay attention to them.
Understanding them brings victory.
Ignoring them means defeat.

DECISION:

*Good strategic
decisions are
based on seeing
how these five
factors together
create your
position.*

Changing trends shape all market positions.
These trends can be obvious or uncertain.
Trends shift between two extreme conditions.
There are patterns in these changes that you can use.

Marketing terrain exists in the minds of customers.
You can reach some customers more easily than others.
Some markets are easier for you than for competitors.
You must know the size and potential of a marketplace.
Choosing the right market determines success or failure.

An organization's decision-making is part of its position.
It requires knowledge, honesty, devotion, courage, and discipline.

Finally, a market position consists of established procedures.
It must include the nature of your distribution channels.
Your policies must be consistent with your mission.
Success requires good marketing techniques.

These five factors completely define your market position.
Make decisions basing strategy upon this position.
Your existing position offers you opportunities.
It is also the source of all your potential problems.

Vision:

Your ability to foresee and leverage changes in the environment is the key to your marketing success.

Leverage:

Your unique marketing opportunities come from your unique position within the larger environment.

You must learn through analysis. 2
You must question the situation.

3You must ask:
Which government has the right philosophy?
Which commander has the skill?
Which season and place has the advantage?
Which method of command works?
Which group of forces has the strength?
Which officers and men have the training?
Which rewards and punishments make sense?
This tells when you will win and when you will lose.
Some commanders perform this analysis.
If you use these commanders, you will win.
Keep them.
Some commanders ignore this analysis.
If you use these commanders, you will lose.
Get rid of them.

Plan an advantage by listening. 3
Adjust to your situation.
Get assistance from the outside.
Influence events.
Then analysis can find opportunities and give you
control.

RELATIVITY:

*No position is
good or bad in
itself. You only
understand
positions by
comparing them
to others.*

2   You learn by researching customers and competitors.
You must know their positions as well as your own.

You must find out:
What are your customers' and competitors' goals?
How do their decision-making processes work?
Where and when are new opportunities arising?
What marketing methods are getting attention?
What are the relative sizes of different markets and organizations?
Which organizations are skillful and which have been lucky?
What features and pricing are successful?
Good research tells you which market segments you can win.
Warrior marketing is based on knowing the market.
Success comes from making decisions based on solid research.
Do only what works.
Many marketing people believe what they want to believe.
Only failure can come from making blind decisions.
Stop doing what doesn't work.

3 Success comes from seeking out new perspectives.
Change how you think about your market position.
Seek opinions from outside your marketplace.
Redefine your market.
New viewpoints uncover new possibilities to easily
advance your position.

MYOPIA:

If you fail to get an outside perspective on your position, you will miss most market opportunities.

Warfare is one thing. 4
It is a philosophy of deception.

³When you are ready, you try to appear incapacitated.
When active, you pretend inactivity.
When you are close to the enemy, you appear distant.
When far away, you pretend you are near.

⁷If the enemy has a strong position, entice him away from it.
If the enemy is confused, be decisive.
If the enemy is solid, prepare against him.
If the enemy is strong, avoid him.
If the enemy is angry, frustrate him.
If the enemy is weaker, make him arrogant.
If the enemy is relaxed, make him work.
If the enemy is united, break him apart.
Attack him when he is unprepared.
Leave when he least expects it.

CONTROL:

*Winning begins
and ends with
the power of
information. You
control others by
controlling their
perceptions.*

¹⁷You will find a place where you can win.
You cannot first signal your intentions.

4 Warrior marketing is simple.
Its mission is controlling the market's perceptions.

You create low expectations so you can easily surpass them.
When you are expanding, you emphasize your stability.
When products are similar, you highlight differences.
When products are different, you highlight similarities.

You can lure customers away from other good alternatives.
You can offer simplicity when competitive choices are confusing.
You can emphasize innovation when competitors emphasize value.
You can emphasize versatility when competitors offer power.
You can mock competitors when they act emotionally.
You can get customers to compare you to your weakest competitors.
You can challenge competitors who are slow to react.
You can lure away your competitors' marketing allies.
Go after markets that competitors have overlooked.
Abandon markets that competitors are concentrating on.

You will find market niches that you can dominate.
You must not promote your dominance in those areas.

DOMINATION:

You can promote products and prices, but you cannot advertise your market position without inviting trouble.

Manage to avoid battle until your organization can **5**
count on certain victory.
You must calculate many advantages.
Before you go to battle, your organization's analysis can indicate that you may not win.
You can count few advantages.
Many advantages add up to victory.
Few advantages add up to defeat.
How can you know your advantages without analyzing them?
We can see where we are by means of our observations.
We can foresee our victory or defeat by planning.

❖ ❖ ❖

PATIENCE:

*Consciously
choosing not
to act is just as
important as
acting decisively
when the time is
right.*

5 Marketing strategy depends on investing only in markets that you are certain to win.

Your analysis must show that the five key factors are in your favor.

To avoid wasting your resources, you must avoid marketing campaigns where the factors are against you.

You must recognize your weaknesses.

Focus your marketing efforts where you are strong.

Avoid marketing campaigns where you are weak.

How can you invest limited market resources without this analysis?

You can know your position only by researching your marketplace.

Decide where to put your marketing efforts based on research.

♦ ♦ ♦

CHOICES:

You advance your position by investing in positions where the five factors are in your favor.

Related Articles from *Sun Tzu's Playbook*

In this first chapter, Sun Tzu introduces the basics of positioning. We explore these ideas in more detail in our Sun Tzu's Art of War Playbook. *To learn the step-by-step techniques for positioning, we recommend the* Playbook *articles listed below.*

1.0.0 Strategic Positioning: developing relatively superior positions.

1.1.0 Position Paths: the continuity of strategic positions over time.

1.1.1 Position Dynamics: how all current positions evolve over time.

1.1.2 Defending Positions: defending current positions until new positions are established.

1.2 Subobjective Positions: the subjective and objective aspects of a position.

1.2.1 Competitive Landscapes: the arenas in which rivals jockey for position.

1.2.2 Exploiting Exploration: how competitive landscapes are searched and positions identified.

1.2.3 Position Complexity: how positions arise from interactions in complex environments.

1.3 Elemental Analysis: the relevant components of all competitive positions.

1.3.1 Competitive Comparison: competition as the comparison of positions.

1.3.2 Element Scalability: how elements of a position scale up to larger positions.

1.4 The External Environment: external conditions shaping strategic positions.

1.4.1 Climate Shift: forces of environmental change shaping temporary conditions.

1.4.2 Ground Features: the persistent resources that we can control.

1.5 Competing Agents: the key characteristics of competitors.

1.5.1 Command Leadership: individual decision-making.

1.5.2. Group Methods: systems for executing decisions.

1.6 Mission Values: the goals and values needed for motivation.

1.6.1 Shared Mission: finding goals that others can share.

1.6.2 Types of Motivations: hierarchies of motivation that define missions.

1.6.3 Shifting Priorities: how missions change according to temporary conditions.

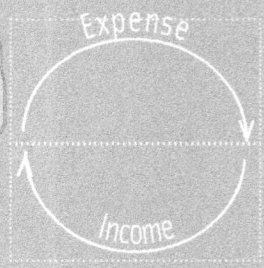

Chapter 2

作戰

Going to War – Targeting

Warrior marketing is an aggressive strategy. It teaches that if you are not actively advancing your market position, your position is actually weakening. Once you understand your market position, you must identify target markets to improve your position.

However, improving your position isn't simply a matter of winning more customers. Warrior marketing specifically defines success as making victory pay. You must win the most profitable markets at the lowest possible cost. This economic focus is one of the reasons that Sun Tzu's strategic system works so well in today's business world.

Picking a target market starts with a fine appreciation of the debilitating cost of marketing and how easily money is wasted. Warrior marketing recognizes that both the total cost and the total reward of marketing are unpredictable. This means that in picking marketing activities you must minimize spending to necessities.

Many physical factors, such as distance, increase your costs. You must choose close, easy targets for your marketing efforts. Warrior marketing makes cost control easy. You must make every marketing campaign pay for itself as directly and quickly as possible to pay for your marketing expenses.

One of the key characteristics of a warrior is discipline. This discipline starts with the ability to control costs. You can only improve your position and cost control at the same time by being very selective about the markets that you target.

SUN TZU SAID:

Everything depends on your use of military philosophy. 1
Moving the army requires thousands of vehicles.
These vehicles must be loaded thousands of times.
The army must carry a huge supply of arms.
You need ten thousand acres of grain.
This results in internal and external shortages.
Any army consumes resources like an invader.
It uses up glue and paint for wood.
It requires armor for its vehicles.
People complain about the waste of a vast amount
of metal.
It will set you back when you attempt to raise tens
of thousands of troops.

ECONOMY:

Strategy teaches that the key to success is making good decisions about using limited resources.

12Using a huge army makes war costly to win.
Long delays create a dull army and sharp defeats.
Attacking enemy cities drains your forces.
Long violent campaigns that exhaust the nation's
resources are wrong.

The Art of Marketing: **Targeting**

A MARKETING WARRIOR HEARS:

1 Everything depends on your marketing goals.
Promoting your products requires thousands of contacts.
Each contact must carry as much information as possible.
Your products must offer a great deal of value.
You need a wealth of resources.
This drains resources from production and sales operations.
Marketing consumes resources like a monster.
It consumes your limited time and energy.
It demands that you defend your market position.
Others complain about how marketing spending consumes cash.
It takes time to build up the distribution channels that marketing depends upon.

Targeting large markets is costly and time-consuming.
Overplanning is not creative and leads to failure.
Targeting tough competitors drains your resources.
Long campaigns that deplete your organization's resources fail too often.

QUICKNESS:

You cannot move quickly if you target big markets with "well-planned" campaigns. This approach is deadly.

AGGRESSION:

Going slowly and "carefully" is more costly and dangerous than moving forward.

[16]Manage a dull army.
You will suffer sharp defeats.
Drain your forces.
Your money will be used up.
Your rivals will multiply as your army collapses
and they will begin against you.
It doesn't matter how smart you are.
You cannot get ahead by taking losses!

[23]You hear of people going to war too quickly.
Still, you won't see a skilled war that lasts a long time.

[25]You can fight a war for a long time or you can make your nation strong.
You can't do both.

Make no assumptions about all the dangers in using **2** military force.
Then you won't make assumptions about the benefits of using arms either.

SMALL IS FAST:

Speed is closely connected to size. Do not mistake costly size for power and safety.

[3]You want to make good use of war.
Do not raise troops repeatedly.
Do not carry too many supplies.
Choose to be useful to your nation.
Feed off the enemy.
Make your army carry only the provisions it needs.

You cannot lose momentum.

If you do, you will lose customers.

You cannot invest everything.

You need to maintain your cash reserves.

If your position weakens, you inspire competitors to come after your customers.

It does not matter how smart you think you are.

You cannot win markets if you lose the initiative.

MOMENTUM:

If marketing does not constantly advance your position, you are inviting attacks on your current position.

You can sometimes go after a new market too soon.

However, the slower your progress, the more often you fail.

You can be slow advancing into new marketplaces, or you can be successful.

You cannot have it both ways.

2 You can never completely insure against failure when you go after a new market.

Nor can you know the total worth of a new marketplace until you have won it.

You want to make good use of your marketing efforts.

Do not throw good money after bad.

Do not try to win more customers than you can sell to.

Support the needs of your company.

Win customers from your competitors.

Spend only the money you absolutely need to spend.

TESTING:

Each move into a new market is a test to see how quickly you can generate money from a new set of customers.

The nation impoverishes itself shipping to troops that **3**
are far away.
Distant transportation is costly for hundreds of families.
Buying goods with the army nearby is also expensive.
High prices also exhaust wealth.
If you exhaust your wealth, you then quickly hollow out your
military.
Military forces consume a nation's wealth entirely.
War leaves households in the former heart of the nation
with nothing.

[8]War destroys hundreds of families.
Out of every ten families, war leaves only seven.
War empties the government's storehouses.
Broken armies will get rid of their horses.
They will throw down their armor, helmets, and arrows.
They will lose their swords and shields.
They will leave their wagons without oxen.
War will consume 60 percent of everything you have.

OPPONENTS:

Because of this, it is the intelligent **4**
commander's duty to feed off the enemy.

*Strategy de-
mands that you
deplete any
resources that
would naturally
go to your com-
petitors.*

[2]Use a cup of the enemy's food.
It is worth twenty of your own.
Win a bushel of the enemy's feed.
It is worth twenty of your own.

3 Marketing to customers who are physically distant is costly for your company.

Transportation increases the price of what you are selling.

Selling into crowded markets cannot be profitable.

Such lack of profit can destroy your company.

Failure is the only result when you waste your resources on unproductive marketing.

Advertising can consume a company's resources entirely.

Marketing expenses can leave the company without profits and worthless.

Bankrupt companies abandon their customers.

Every year, a large percentage of businesses fail.

Misguided marketing depletes a company's resources.

Failed marketing forces companies to abandon their assets.

These companies lose customers, employees, and investors.

These companies lose their inventory and buildings.

They lose their machinery and vehicles.

Poor marketing can negate the total value of a company.

4 For these reasons, you must go after markets that generate money quickly for your company.

Take a dollar in sales today.

It is worth twenty dollars in sales tomorrow.

Take a dollar from your competitor's customer.

It is worth twenty dollars of market potential.

RESULTS:

Choose target customers from whom you can quickly generate profits to pay for more marketing to them.

⁶You can kill the enemy and frustrate him as well.
Take the enemy's strength from him by stealing away his
money.

⁸Fight for the enemy's supply wagons.
Capture his supplies by using overwhelming force.
Reward the first who capture them.
Then change their banners and flags.
Mix them in with your own wagons to increase your supply
line.
Keep your soldiers strong by providing for them.
This is what it means to beat the enemy while you grow
more powerful.

Make victory in war pay for itself. **5**
Avoid expensive, long campaigns.
The military commander's knowledge is the key.
It determines if the civilian officials can govern.
It determines if the nation's households are peaceful or a
danger to the state.

MAKE IT PAY:

Success is de-
fined only by its
profitability.

You must win customers away from your competitors.
You win market share by taking away money that would have gone to your rivals.

Marketing must generate profits.
Focus your marketing on winning sales dollars.
Reward the first customers who come to you.
Use existing customers to bring in more customers.
Base your future marketing budgets solely on past success in the market.
Expanding your successes makes you successful.
This is what it means to win a market while growing more influential.

5 Win market segments that can pay for themselves.
Avoid long, expensive marketing campaigns.
Knowing your customers is the key.
Your knowledge determines your profitability.
Your knowledge determines whether marketing efforts are productive or destructive to your organization.

✦ ✦ ✦

CAMPAIGNS:

Choose close,
inexpensive, and
small targets.

Related Articles from *Sun Tzu's Playbook*

In his second chapter, Sun Tzu teaches basic competitive economics. We explore these ideas in more detail in our **Sun Tzu's Art of War Playbook** *To learn the step-by-step techniques for economical political campaigning, we recommend the articles listed below.*

1.3.1 Competitive Comparison: competition as the comparison of positions.

1.6.1 Shared Mission: finding goals that others can share.

1.8.3 Cycle Time: speed in feedback and reaction.

1.8.4 Probabilistic Process: the role of chance in strategic processes and systems.

2.2.1 Personal Relationships: how information depends on personal relationships.

2.2.2 Mental Models: how mental models simplify decision-making.

2.3.4 Using Questions: using questions in gathering information and predicting reactions.

3.1 Strategic Economics: balancing the cost and benefits of positioning.

3.1.1 Resource Limitations: the inherent limitation of strategic resources.

3.1.2 Strategic Profitability: understanding gains and losses.

3.1.3 Conflict Cost: the costly nature of resolving competitive comparisons by conflict.

3.1.4 Openings: seeking openings to avoid costly conflict.

3.1.5 Unpredictable Value: the limitations of predicting the value of positions.

3.1.6 Time Limitations: the time limits on opportunities.

4.0 Leveraging Probability: better decisions regarding our choice of opportunities.

4.1 Future Potential: the limitations and potential of current and future positions.

4.2 Choosing Non-Action: choosing between action and non-action.

5.3 Reaction Time: the use of speed in choosing actions.

5.3.1 Speed and Quickness: the use of pace within a dynamic environment.

5.3.2 Opportunity Windows: the effect of speed upon opposition.

5.3.3 Information Freshness: choosing actions based on freshness of information.

5.4 Minimizing Action: minimizing waste, i.e., less is more.

5.4.1 Testing Value : choosing actions to test for value.

5.4.2 Successful Mistakes: learning from our mistakes.

5.5 Focused Power: size consideration in safe experimentation.

5.5.1 Force Size: limiting the size of force in an advance.

5.5.2 Distance Limitations: the use of short steps to reach distant goals.

Uniting

Dissolve

Focusing

Chapter 3

謀攻

Planning Attacks – Focus

After you identify the best possible target market, you must then start focusing on the market. Warrior marketing demands concentration of resources. In the science of strategy, this focus demands the unity of the entire organization. Profits are the purpose of marketing, but profits cannot be generated by marketing alone. Any marketing campaign is doomed unless you have the whole organization united in its concentration on the target market.

Focus requires the cooperation of every part of the organization. It affects every level of an organization. The goal is not just to make your penetration of the market successful but to make it successful without generating costly conflict.

In classical strategy, an attack is not fighting with an opponent. It is moving into a new territory. There are four different forms of attack, so there are four different ways you can focus on your target market. Some of these methods are much better than others.

Progress is made with small steps. Each step is a concentrated battle in which you have the clear advantage. The relative strength of competitors determines your tactics at each step.

Internal politics is the most deadly enemy of focus. You must know five things as the marketing manager to avoid divisive, destructive internal politics. In the end, your success depends on your ability to correctly calculate what resources you can focus on the target market. If you cannot focus on it better than the competition can, it is best to leave that market alone.

The Art of War: **Planning Attacks**

SUN TZU SAID:

Everyone relies on the arts of war. 1
A united nation is strong.
A divided nation is weak.
A united army is strong.
A divided army is weak.
A united force is strong.
A divided force is weak.
United men are strong.
Divided men are weak.
A united unit is strong.
A divided unit is weak.

[12]Unity works because it enables you to win every battle you fight.
Still, this is the foolish goal of a weak leader.
Avoid battle and make the enemy's men surrender.
This is the right goal for a superior leader.

The best way to make war is to ruin the enemy's plans. 2
The next best is to disrupt alliances.
The next best is to attack the opposing army.
The worst is to attack the enemy's cities.

The Art of Marketing: **Focus**

1 All businesses have a marketing strategy.
A focused campaign works.
An unfocused campaign does not.
A single concept is easy to sell.
Many concepts are hard to sell.
A concentrated effort is successful.
A divided effort fails.
A small market is simple.
A spread-out market is difficult.
A single message works.
Multiple messages do not work.

FOCUS:

*A market-
ing campaign
depends upon a
, clear focused
message.*

Focus works because it enables you to beat the competition in every segment you target.
This still does not make you a great marketing manager.
You want to win market segments without competition.
This is your most important goal.

2 It is best to focus on markets before competitors can.
The next best method is to focus on your competitors' supporters.
The next best is to focus on outmaneuvering your competitors.
The worst method is to focus on entrenched competitive positions.

ATTACKS:

In classical strategy, an attack is any form of invading an opponent's territory. It is not fighting with competitors.

5This is what happens when you attack a city.
You can attempt it, but you can't finish it.
First you must make siege engines.
You need the right equipment and machinery.
It takes three months and still you cannot win.
Then you try to encircle the area.
You use three more months without making progress.
Your command still doesn't succeed and this angers you.
You then try to swarm the city.
This kills a third of your officers and men.
You are still unable to draw the enemy out of the city.
This attack is a disaster.

Make good use of war. 3
Make the enemy's troops surrender.
You can do this fighting only minor battles.
You can draw their men out of their cities.
You can do it with small attacks.
You can destroy the men of a nation.
You must keep your campaign short.

DECISION:

Good strategic decisions are based on seeing how these five factors together create your position.

8You must use total war, fighting with everything you have.
Never stop fighting when at war.
You can gain complete advantage.
To do this, you must plan your strategy of attack.

What happens when you focus on an entrenched product position?
You can invest in marketing, but you cannot win sales.
First, you must prepare the superior product offering.
You need to buy advertising and build distribution.
This takes months and doesn't work.
You must do all that your competitor does, only better.
After more months of work, you will not win away its customers.
Your marketing doesn't result in sales and everyone pressures you.
You get desperate and invest all your resources at once.
This does permanent damage to your organization.
You are still unable to damage the competitor's established position.
This type of focus is a waste of resources.

Disaster:

Simply copying competitors' best products and best market successes is a costly disaster just waiting to happen.

3 Make good use of competition.
Let competitors surrender market segments to you.
You can do it without a single battle.
You can win customers away from their current suppliers.
You do it by focusing on small groups of people.
You can win away your competitors' customers.
You must move quickly into the market.

In marketing, you must leverage every possible resource to create sales.
Never stop selling when you go after a segment.
You can win customers if you focus your attention.
To do this, you must know your marketing strategy.

Leverage:

Your real marketing opportunities come from your unique position within the larger environment.

[12]The rules for making war are:
If you outnumber enemy forces ten to one, surround them.
If you outnumber them five to one, attack them.
If you outnumber them two to one, divide them.
If you are equal, then find an advantageous battle.
If you are fewer, defend against them.
If you are much weaker, evade them.

[19]Small forces are not powerful.
However, large forces cannot catch them.

You must master command. 4
The nation must support you.

[3]Supporting the military makes the nation powerful.
Not supporting the military makes the nation weak.

[5]The army's position is made more difficult by politicians in
three different ways.
Ignorant of the whole army's inability to advance, they
order an advance.
Ignorant of the whole army's inability to withdraw, they
order a withdrawal.
We call this tying up the army.
Politicians don't understand the army's business.
Still, they think they can run an army.
This confuses the army's officers.

The Art of Marketing: **Focus**

You must focus more resources on the market than competitors do.
If your resources are ten times bigger, you isolate competitors.
If your resources are five times bigger, you challenge them directly.
If your resources are twice as large, refocus on a smaller segment.
If your resources are equal, sell only to the most profitable markets.
If your resources are smaller, defend existing customers.
If your resources are much smaller, find small market niches.

Small companies cannot sell to broad markets.
However, large companies cannot satisfy niche markets.

4 Your company must dominate its market segments.
Your organization must support you.

Focusing on its market makes a company competitive.
Spreading out in broad general markets makes a company weak.

Sales management can create problems in the market in three different ways.
Ignorant of which market segments are winnable, salespeople go after any customer.
Ignorant of which markets segments cannot be won, salespeople forget existing customers.
This approach wastes your marketing effort.
Sales management does not understand marketing.
Salespeople think that they should go after any customer.
This confuses your marketing focus.

[12]Politicians don't know the army's chain of command.
They give the army too much freedom.
This will create distrust among the army's officers.

[15]The entire army becomes confused and distrusting.
This invites invasion by many different rivals.
We say correctly that disorder in an army kills victory.

You must know five things to win: **5**
Victory comes from knowing when to attack and when to avoid battle.
Victory comes from correctly using both large and small forces.
Victory comes from everyone sharing the same goals.
Victory comes from finding opportunities in problems.
Victory comes from having a capable commander and the government leaving him alone.
You must know these five things.
You then know the theory of victory.

We say: **6**
"Know yourself and know your enemy.
You will be safe in every battle.
You may know yourself but not know the enemy.
You will then lose one battle for every one you win.
You may not know yourself or the enemy.
You will then lose every battle."

The Art of Marketing: **Focus**

Sales management does not understand marketing priorities.
Sales managers give their people too much freedom.
This creates uncertainty in your market focus.

If you confuse your target customers, you create distrust.
This invites competitors to win away your customers.
An unfocused campaign destroys your chances of success.

5 You must know five things to focus on a market.
You must know when to invest in a given market segment and when
to save your money.
You must concentrate on a market of the appropriate size—one that
fits the size of your organization.
You must unite your organization in its desire to win that market.
You must know how to turn problems into opportunities.
You must prioritize the organization's decisions and stop manage-
ment from second-guessing itself.
You must know these five things.
You then know the philosophy of winning campaigns.

6 Experience says:
Know your capabilities and your target market.
If you do, you can easily win any competitive challenge.
You can know your capabilities but not your market.
Then, for every successful campaign you will waste another.
You can know neither your capabilities nor your market.
Then you will lose every campaign.

✦ ✦ ✦

Related Articles from *Sun Tzu's Playbook*

In this third chapter, Sun Tzu introduces the basics of advancing into new areas. To learn the step-by-step techniques involved, we recommend the Sun Tzu's Art of War Playbook *articles listed below.*

1.1.1 Position Dynamics: how all current positions are always getting better or worse.

1.1.2 Defending Positions: how we defend our current positions until new positions are established.

1.2 Subobjective Positions: the subjective and objective aspects of a position.

1.3.1 Competitive Comparison: competition as the comparison of positions.

1.7 Competitive Power: the sources of superiority in challenges.

1.7.1 Team Unity: strength by joining with others.

1.7.2 Goal Focus: strength as arising from concentrating efforts.

1.8 Progress Cycle: the adaptive loop by which positions are advanced.

1.8.1 Creation and Destruction: the creation and destruction of competitive positions.

1.8.2 The Adaptive Loop: the continual reiteration of position analysis.

2.3.6 Promises and Threats: the use of promises and threats as strategic moves.

2.4 Contact Networks: the range of contacts needed to create perspective.

2.4.1 Ground Perspective: getting information on a new competitive arena.

2.4.2 Climate Perspective: getting perspective on temporary external conditions.

3.0.0 Identifying Opportunities: the use of opportunities to advance a position.

3.1.3 Conflict Cost: the costly nature of resolving competitive comparisons by conflict.

3.2 Opportunity Creation: how change creates opportunities.

3.2.2 Opportunity Invisibility: why opportunities are always hidden.

3.2.4 Emptiness and Fullness: the transformations between strength and weakness.

3.4 Dis-Economies of Scale: how opportunities are created by the size of others.

3.4.2 Opportunity Fit: finding new opportunities that fit your size.

3.4.3 Reaction Lag: how size creates temporary openings.

3.5 Strength and Weakness: openings created by the strength of others.

3.6 Leveraging Subjectivity: openings between subjective and objective positions.

3.7 Defining the Ground: redefining a competitive arena to create relative mismatches.

5.6 Defensive Advances: balancing defending and advancing positions.

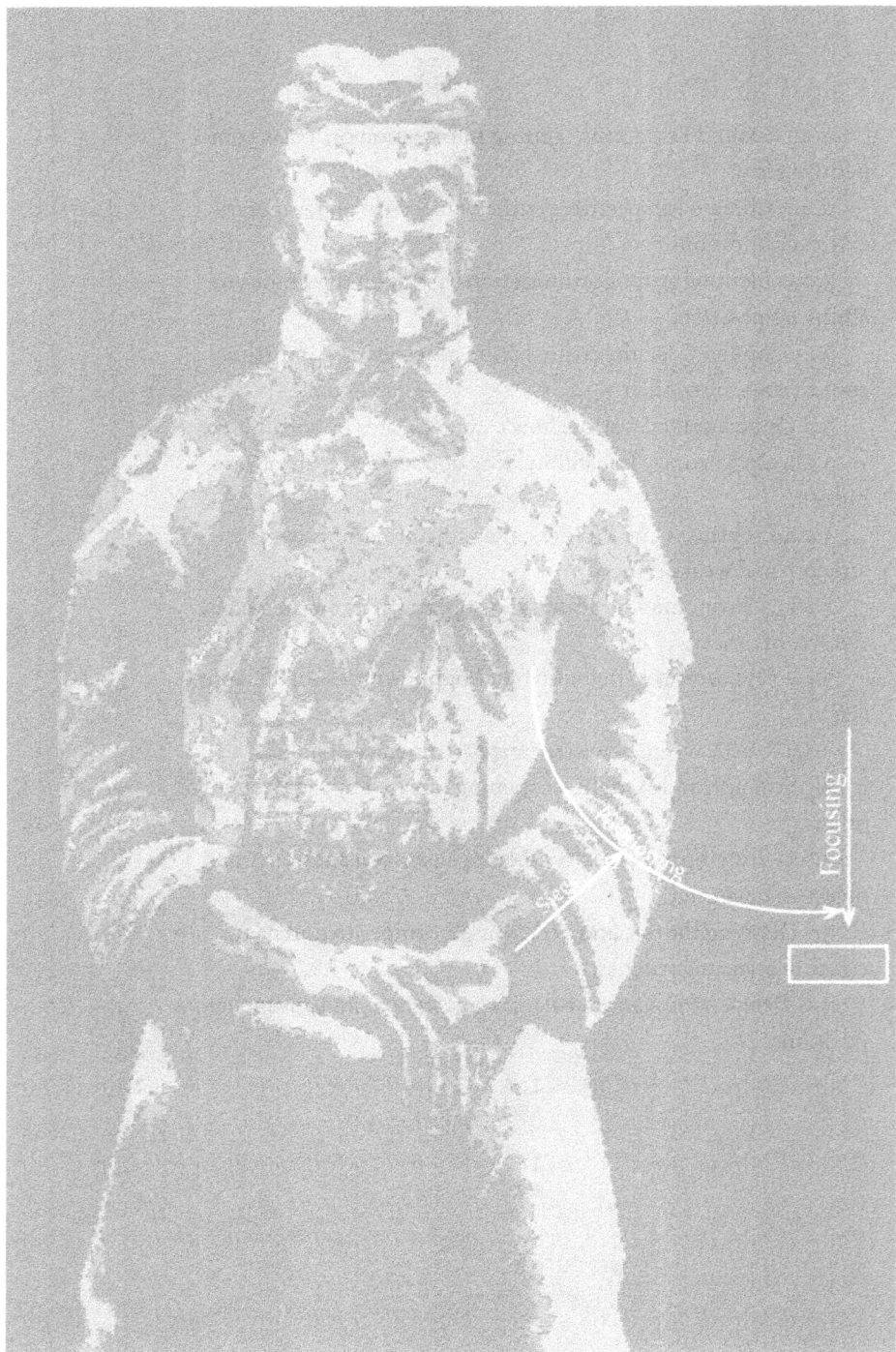

Chapter 4

形

Positioning – Branding

Warrior marketing is a strategy of taking advantage of the opportunities that you are given. You do not create a brand simply by doing some fancy graphics and spending a lot of money on advertising to get your message out. Brands and market positions do not arise miraculously out of the minds of marketing geniuses. They are made possible by your current position and the openings around you in the marketplace. The skill of positioning is recognizing these opportunities and knowing how to take advantage of them.

Until you see an unsatisfied need in the marketplace, you can do no more than protect your existing position; only the competitive environment itself can create new opportunities for you. Until you find that opening, you must concentrate on defending your existing position and brand identity.

When you recognize an opportunity, the problem becomes one of execution. Taking advantage of a new position requires moving the entire organization from one way of presenting itself to another. This challenge is not only internal. Your new position is likely to be challenged by competitors who want to take advantage of the same opportunity. You must calculate beforehand your likelihood of winning the position you desire.

Positioning and branding are much more than labels on packages and an advertising campaign. Branding gives people in the marketplace a new way of seeing themselves. Done correctly, branding makes it easy for customers to buy.

The Art of War: Positioning

Learn from the history of successful battles. 1
Your first actions should deny victory to the enemy.
You pay attention to your enemy to find the way to
win.
You alone can deny victory to the enemy.
Only your enemy can allow you to win.

DEFENSE:

Strategy dictates that you must first make sure that your existing position is secure before moving to a new one.

[6]You must fight well.
You can prevent the enemy's victory.
You cannot win unless the enemy enables your
victory.

[9]We say:
You see the opportunity for victory; you don't
create it.

The Art of Marketing: **Branding**

A MARKETING WARRIOR HEARS:

1 Learn what works in meeting market competition.
You first protect your existing brand from competitors.
You then look for openings that allow you to advance your
brand in the market.
You can protect your customers from competitors.
Competitors must allow you to win their customers.

You must target your brand clearly.
You can prevent competitors' success.
You cannot advance your brand without using com-
petitors' weaknesses against them.

The truth is:
You must discover the opportunity for a brand identity; you do not create it.

OPENINGS:

*Branding must
take advantage
of opportunities
in the market-
place that your
competitors
create for you.*

You are sometimes unable to win. 2
You must then defend.
You will eventually be able to win.
You must then attack.
Defend when you have insufficient strength.
Attack when you have a surplus of strength.

7You must defend yourself well.
Save your forces and dig in.
You must attack well.
Move your forces when you have a clear advantage.

11You must always protect yourself until you can completely triumph.

Some may see how to win. 3
However, they cannot position their forces where they must.
This demonstrates limited ability.

4Some can struggle to a victory and the whole world may praise their winning.
This also demonstrates a limited ability.

6Win as easily as picking up a fallen hair.
Don't use all of your forces.
See the time to move.
Don't try to find something clever.
Hear the clap of thunder.
Don't try to hear something subtle.

2 You cannot always see a new product position.
So concentrate on your existing customers.
You will eventually discover an opening in the market.
Then shape your brand to fit into it.
Maintain your brand when you lack the resources to expand.
Expand only when you have more resources than you need.

You must defend your existing brand identity.
Conserve your resources and dig in.
You must also advance your brand.
Reshape your brand identity to take advantage of opportunities.

Maintain your market share until you are certain you have found an opening to advance it.

3 You may see opportunities in the marketplace.
Yet you do not see how to brand your product to win them.
This shows a limited ability.

You can create a market identity by investing a great deal of time and money.
This also shows a limited ability.

Expanding only makes sense when it is easy.
Avoid trying to buy a market position.
Watch for a clear opportunity.
Creating a brand is not a matter of gimmicks.
Hear what customers say they want.
Do not imagine desires that are hidden.

[12]Learn from the history of successful battles.
Victory goes to those who make winning easy.
A good battle is one that you will obviously win.
It doesn't take intelligence to win a reputation.
It doesn't take courage to achieve success.

[17]You must win your battles without effort.
Avoid difficult struggles.
Fight when your position must win.
You always win by preventing your defeat.

[21]You must engage only in winning battles.
Position yourself where you cannot lose.
Never waste an opportunity to defeat your enemy.

[24]You win a war by first assuring yourself of victory.
Only afterward do you look for a fight.
Outmaneuver the enemy before the first battle and then
fight to win.

BATTLE:

*In classical
strategy, battle
means meeting
an opponent's
challenge, not
necessarily a
fight.*

Learn from your successful efforts.
Markets go to those who make buying easy.
A good brand is one that will obviously satisfy customers.
You are foolish if you just want to get your name known.
You can be successful by minimizing your risks.

You want to grow your brand without fighting for customers.
Avoid challenging competitors.
Redefine product categories so you are the clear leader.
You win customers by being the best at providing what they need.

You must invest only in valuable brand positions.
Create an image that cannot fail.
Never pass by an opportunity to win the competition's customers.

You win markets by discovering winning brand positions.
Only after discovery do you invest in building the brand.
You must identify the right product position and then work to
create the appropriate brand identity.

IDENTITY:

*The market
needs to know
who you are but
only in terms of
what you can
do to meet its
needs.*

You must make good use of war. 4
Study military philosophy and the art of defense.
You can control your victory or defeat.

4This is the art of war:
"1.   Discuss the distances.
2.   Discuss your numbers.
3.   Discuss your calculations.
4.   Discuss your decisions.
5.   Discuss victory.

10The ground determines the distance.
The distance determines your numbers.
Your numbers determine your calculations.
Your calculations determine your decisions.
Your decisions determine your victory."

15Creating a winning war is like balancing a coin of gold
against a coin of silver.
Creating a losing war is like balancing a coin of silver
against a coin of gold.

Winning a battle is always a matter of people. 5
You pour them into battle like a flood of
water pouring into a deep gorge.
This is a matter of positioning.

✦ ✦ ✦

4 You must make use of marketing strategy.
Know your marketing goals and how to defend your markets.
You alone determine your success or failure.

Warrior marketing requires that you:
1.   Discuss market barriers to entry.
2.   Discuss the required investment.
3.   Discuss the potential profits.
4.   Discuss your brand positioning.
5.   Discuss your likelihood of success.

Customer needs determine the barriers to entry.
These barriers determine the required investment.
The investment required determines the potential profit.
The potential profit determines your brand positioning.
Your brand positioning determines your success.

Creating a successful brand position is matter of being the best in a
specific area rather than the second best.
Creating a losing brand position is matter of focusing on areas
where you are the second best choice.

5 Expanding your position depends on knowing customers.
You must take advantage of people's desire to try
new ways to address unsatisfied needs.
This is the basis for product branding.

✦ ✦ ✦

Related Articles from *Sun Tzu's Playbook*

In this fourth chapter, Sun Tzu explains the process for advancing positions. To learn the step-by-step techniques involved, we recommend the Sun Tzu's Art of War Playbook *articles listed below.*

1.1.2 Defending Positions: how we defend our current positions until new positions are established.

1.2 Subobjective Positions: the subjective and objective aspects of a position.

1.3.1 Competitive Comparison: competition as the comparison of positions.

1.7 Competitive Power: the sources of superiority in challenges.

1.8 Progress Cycle: the adaptive loop by which positions are advanced.

1.8.1 Creation and Destruction: the creation and destruction of competitive positions.

1.8.2 The Adaptive Loop: the continual reiteration of position analysis.

3.0.0 Identifying Opportunities: the use of opportunities to advance a position.

3.2 Opportunity Creation: how change creates opportunities.

Chapter 5

势

Momentum – Creativity

Marketing programs must continually change or they grow stale, but they cannot change too much or they confuse the marketplace. Warrior marketing is a system for producing constant improvements that both create and preserve market momentum.

Creativity does not take place in a vacuum. Creativity relies upon a solid base of established brand identity. It is a mistake to attempt reinventing your market programs from scratch. Success is a matter of putting together established, proven ideas and images with new, surprising elements. Predictable products and services make customers comfortable, but they must be combined with new and interesting ideas to keep them interesting and fresh.

There are an infinite number of innovative marketing ideas that you can use to maintain your market momentum. Creativity is a matter of combining existing elements in a new or unusual way. Warrior marketing works with a limited palette of sounds, colors, and tastes, but it continually rearranges those elements to constantly refocus the brand identity and position.

Market timing is a matter of using creative changes at the appropriate moment to reap the best rewards. The best marketing programs build up tension in the marketplace that is released by the unveiling of a new product, promotion, or price.

The maintenance of momentum and the use of timing allows you some control over unpredictable markets. Momentum is a powerful force in controlling people's perceptions and attitudes.

The Art of War: **Momentum**

SUN TZU SAID:

You control a large group the same as you control a few. 1
You just divide their ranks correctly.
You fight a large army the same as you fight a small one.
You only need the right position and communication.
You may meet a large enemy army.
You must be able to sustain an enemy attack without being defeated.
You must correctly use both surprise and direct action.
Your army's position must increase your strength.
Troops flanking an enemy can smash them like eggs.
You must correctly use both strength and weakness.

It is the same in all battles. 2
You use a direct approach to engage the enemy.
You use surprise to win.

STANDARDS:

Momentum requires developing a set of standards that customers can depend upon.

4You must use surprise for a successful invasion.
Surprise is as infinite as the weather and land.
Surprise is as inexhaustible as the flow of a river.

The Art of Marketing: Creativity

A MARKETING WARRIOR HEARS:

1 You win large markets in the same way as small ones.
You need only to divide them into the right segments.
You win large customers the same way you win small ones.
You need the right brand identity and market message.
You will be challenged by larger competitors.
You must maintain a brand identity that can always withstand a competitive challenge.
You must use both innovation and proven practices.
You must constantly strengthen your market position.
You find new angles to keep competitors off-balance.
You must see both their strengths and weaknesses.

2 All marketing challenges are the same.
You meet a competitive challenge by being dependable.
You beat competitors by being innovative.

Use creativity to win new market segments.
There are an infinite number of new marketing ideas.
Creativity harnesses the flow of change in the world.

INNOVATION:

Innovation of standards creates a moving target that competitors cannot easily attack.

⁷You can be stopped and yet recover the initiative.
You must use your days and months correctly.

⁹If you are defeated, you can recover.
You must use the four seasons correctly.

¹¹There are only a few notes in the scale.
Yet you can always rearrange them.
You can never hear every song of victory.

¹⁴There are only a few basic colors.
Yet you can always mix them.
You can never see all the shades of victory.

¹⁷There are only a few flavors.
Yet you can always blend them.
You can never taste all the flavors of victory.

²⁰You fight with momentum.
There are only a few types of surprises and direct actions.
Yet you can always vary the ones you use.
There is no limit to the ways you can win.

²⁴Surprise and direct action give birth to each other.
They are like a circle without end.
You cannot exhaust all their possible combinations!

Surging waters flow together rapidly. 3
Its pressure washes away boulders.
This is momentum.

Yesterday's disappointments can become tomorrow's successes.
You must work out the problems over time.

You can make mistakes and still recover.
Use the market's trends correctly.

You must rely on a few clear marketing messages.
But you can rearrange them any number of ways.
You can always find a better way to communicate your value.

You must rely on a few established brand images.
But you can combine those images in new ways.
You will never exhaust all the subtle differences in value.

You must appeal to only a few types of customer tastes.
Yet they can be put together in any number of ways.
You will never discover all the permutations of value.

You win markets with momentum.
Momentum comes from mixing new ideas with proven standards.
You can combine both to make each campaign unique.
You can advance your position in any number of ways.

Creativity and standards depend on each other.
Standards inspire creativity, which sets new standards.
Using both, you can always improve your brand's position.

3 Small advances add up quickly.
The pressure of constant change reduces customer resistance.
This is marketing momentum.

4A hawk suddenly strikes a bird.
Its contact alone kills the prey.
This is timing.

7You must fight only winning battles.
Your momentum must be overwhelming.
Your timing must be exact.

10Your momentum is like the tension of a bent crossbow.
Your timing is like the pulling of a trigger.

War is very complicated and confusing. 4
Battle is chaotic.
Nevertheless, you must not allow chaos.

4War is very sloppy and messy.
Positions turn around.
Nevertheless, you must never be defeated.

7Chaos gives birth to control.
Fear gives birth to courage.
Weakness gives birth to strength.

MOMENTUM:

Dependable standards and constant improvement create pressure in the marketplace to buy.

10You must control chaos.
This depends on your planning.
Your men must brave their fears.
This depends on momentum.

14You have strengths and weaknesses.
These come from your position.

Good promotions catch competitors unprepared.
The surprise alone puts them at a disadvantage.
Promotion is a matter of timing.

You must invest only in marketing that wins sales.
The pressure for customers to buy must increase over time.
You promote only when the time is right.

Market momentum increases the pressure to buy.
Promotion makes it easy to buy now.

4 Markets are complex and uncertain.
You meet unpredictable challenges.
Warrior marketing gives you a sense of control.

Marketing is never neat and tidy.
Brand positions are constantly shifting.
You must defend your market position.

The market's uncertainty demands your clarity.
The market's fear demands your certainty.
The market's weakness gives you an opportunity.

Clarify the confusion in the marketplace.
Your analysis of the market must simplify it.
Give customers the confidence to buy.
Momentum makes buying easy.

Every brand appeals to some and not to others.
Position your brand to appeal to the right customers.

TIMING:

Promotion releases the pressure created by momentum to give customers a reason to buy now.

[16]You must force the enemy to move to your advantage.

Use your position.

The enemy must follow you.

Surrender a position.

The enemy must take it.

You can offer an advantage to move him.

You can use your men to move him.

You can use your strength to hold him.

You want a successful battle. 5

To do this, you must seek momentum.

Do not just demand a good fight from your people.

You must pick good people and then give them momentum.

[5]You must create momentum.

You create it with your men during battle.

This is comparable to rolling trees and stones.

Trees and stones roll because of their shape and weight.

Offer men safety and they will stay calm.

Endanger them and they will act.

Give them a place and they will hold.

Round them up and they will march.

[13]You make your men powerful in battle with momentum.

This should be like rolling round stones down over a high,

steep cliff.

Momentum is critical.

✦ ✦ ✦

The Art of Marketing: **Creativity**

You must create new categories in customers' minds.
Leverage your existing brand.
Competitors must adjust to you.
Give up your least valuable customers.
You want these customers to identify with your competition.
You adjust your prices to win the right customers.
You adjust your features to win the right customers.
Use your organization to keep customers happy.

5 You want to dominate your markets.
To maintain dominance, you must constantly improve.
You cannot just demand better marketing ideas from your people.
You pick the best people and teach them standards and innovation.

You want to generate market pressure.
Insist that your people challenge your competition.
You put pressure along the path of least resistance.
Market ideas work because they leverage market conditions.
Offer customers dependability and they will stay with you.
Deal with the threats customers feel and they come to you.
Customers need clear market positions that they can hold on to.
Gather customers together and they will follow you.

Your brand will beat competitors if it has the momentum.
You must take advantage of people's desire to
follow the path of least resistance.
People need pressure.

♦ ♦ ♦

Related Articles from *Sun Tzu's Playbook*

In his fifth chapter, Sun Tzu explains the process for creating momentum. To learn the step-by-step techniques involved, we recommend the Sun Tzu's Art of War Playbook articles listed below.

1.2 Subobjective Positions: the subjective and objective aspects of a position.

7.0 Creating Momentum: how momentum requires creativity.

7.1 Order from Chaos: the value of chaos in creating competitive momentum.

7.1.1 Creating Surprise: creating surprise using our chaotic environment.

7.1.2 Momentum Psychology: the psychology of surprise.

7.1.3 Standards and Innovation: the methodology of creativity.

7.2 Standards First: the role of standards in creating connections with others.

7.2.1 Proven Methods: identifying and recognizing the limits of best practices.

7.2.2 Preparing Expectations: how we shape other people's expectations.

7.3 Strategic Innovation: a simple system for innovation.

7.3.1 Expected Elements: dividing processes and systems into components.

Chapter 6

虛 實

Weakness and Strength — Needs and Satisfaction

Strategy teaches that no market or market position is perfect. Every choice of brand identity has both advantages and disadvantages. These strengths and weaknesses are two sides of the same coin. There are always some customer needs that are satisfied and other needs that go unsatisfied.

The first to address customer needs that remain unsatisfied always has a strategic advantage. It is always faster and easier to compete on the basis of what competitors are *not* doing than on the basis of what competitors are already doing well. You can move into new markets more quickly when no one else is addressing the needs of that market. When you are a "first mover" into a new area, you have time to build up a defensible market position.

When a marketing campaign targets an unexplored market, you need to keep your plans a secret. You do not want your competitors to know where you are planning to move. In exploiting holes in the marketplace, you are identifying needs that others have not satisfied. You do not want to alert your competitors to these opportunities until it is too late for them to counter your moves.

Warrior marketing balances the need for creating market awareness against the need to keep competitors in the dark. You want to communicate in arenas where customers can hear you but competitors cannot.

There is no perfect plan, action, position, or competitor, but the goal is to leverage your strengths against competitive weakness.

The Art of War: **Weakness and Strength**

Sun Tzu said:

Always arrive first to the empty battlefield to await the 1
enemy at your leisure.
After the battleground is occupied and you hurry to it, fighting is more difficult.

3You want a successful battle.
Move your men, but not into opposing forces.

5You can make the enemy come to you.
Offer him an advantage.
You can make the enemy avoid coming to you.
Threaten him with danger.

WEAKNESS:

9When the enemy is fresh, you can tire him.
When he is well fed, you can starve him.
When he is relaxed, you can move him.

*Competitors'
weaknesses
arise naturally
from unsatisfied
customer needs.
Needs create
opportunities.*

The Art of Marketing: Needs and Satisfaction

A MARKETING WARRIOR HEARS:

1 You want the advantage of getting to the market before the competition does.
Avoid attacking markets where the competition is already entrenched.

Your only goal is to make money.
Find your own markets; do not follow the competition.

You can entice customers away from competitors.
Satisfy needs that others do not.
You can stop competitors from copying you.
Design offers that are costly for them to duplicate.

Every customer's happiness is only temporary.
Every customer's satisfaction creates new needs.
Any customer's inertia can be turned into action.

STRENGTHS:

Every competitor has areas of strength that make some offerings easier for them than others.

Leave any place without haste. 2
Hurry to where you are unexpected.
You can easily march hundreds of miles without tiring.
To do so, travel through areas that are deserted.
You must take whatever you attack.
Attack when there is no defense.
You must have walls to defend.
Defend where it is impossible to attack.

AVOIDANCE:

Success depends upon avoiding competitive challenges while you move to develop better positions.

9Be skilled in attacking.
Give the enemy no idea where to defend.

11Be skillful in your defense.
Give the enemy no idea where to attack.

Be subtle! Be subtle! 3
Arrive without any clear formation.
Ghostly! Ghostly!
Arrive without a sound.
You must use all your skill to control the enemy's decisions.

6Advance where he can't defend.
Charge through his openings.
Withdraw where the enemy cannot chase you.
Move quickly so that he cannot catch you.

10Always pick your own battles.

2 Abandon any established marketplaces slowly.
Be the first to get into a new marketplace.
You establish positions easily when no competitors are in a market.
Move quickly into areas where needs are overlooked.
Address the problems that you find.
Make offers that competitors cannot easily duplicate.
Create barriers to entry to protect new markets.
Satisfy customers that competitors cannot satisfy.

Be clever about winning customers.
Find needs that competitors have overlooked.

Be smart about keeping customers.
Leave no unmet needs for competitors to exploit.

> SPECIALIZE:
>
> *Focus your marketing on products and market positions that are difficult for competitors to duplicate.*

3 Change market positions gradually.
Do not let competitors know your plan.
Keep quiet within your industry.
Move into new markets quietly.
Communicate narrowly to customers so competitors can't react.

Sell to market areas where competitors have limitations.
Aggressively fill the gaps that competitors leave.
Pull back into markets where there are barriers to entry.
Change your offerings so competitors cannot copy you.

Target your own specialized niches.

The enemy can hide behind high walls and deep trenches.
Do not try to win by fighting him directly.
Instead, attack a place that he must recapture.
Avoid the battles that you don't want.
You can divide the ground and yet defend it.
Don't give the enemy anything to win.
Divert him by coming to where you defend.

Make other men take a position while you take none. 4
Then focus your forces where the enemy divides his forces.
Where you focus, you unite your forces.
When the enemy divides, he creates many small groups.
You want your large group to attack one of his small ones.
Then you have many men where the enemy has but a few.
Your larger force can overwhelm his smaller one.
Then go on to the next small enemy group.
You can take them one at a time.

You must keep the place that you have chosen as a 5
battleground a secret.
The enemy must not know.
Force the enemy to prepare his defense in many
places.
You want the enemy to defend many places.
Then you can choose where to fight.
His forces will be weak there.

SECRECY:

You cannot exploit the weakness of your opponents if everyone knows what you are doing.

Your competitors are well entrenched in their markets.
You cannot beat them by going after these markets directly.
Instead, find the customers that they are serving poorly.
Fighting for customers is never profitable.
You can divide the market to create a protected segment.
Do not leave needs in that market for others to address.
Distract competitors from coming after your customers.

4 See where competitors are before you move.
Focus on the gaps in their marketing efforts.
When you focus, you concentrate your resources.
When competitors divide their attention, they create needs.
You must focus your marketing efforts on those unmet needs.
You can dominate any segment if others ignore it.
You can easily make good profits in any overlooked segments.
You can then move on to the next neglected segment.
Tackle them one at a time.

5 You must keep your market focus a secret from your competitors.
It will tempt them if they know.
You want to encourage competitors to sell to every possible segment.
They must market themselves too broadly.
You can then choose the segments that you want.
Competition will be weak there.

ADAPTABILITY:

Marketing is not the execution of some grand plan but constantly adjusting to openings in the marketplace.

⁷If he reinforces his front lines, he depletes his rear.
If he reinforces his rear, he depletes his front.
If he reinforces his right flank, he depletes his left.
If he reinforces his left flank, he depletes his right.
Without knowing the place of attack, he cannot
prepare.
Without knowing the right place, he will be weak
everywhere.

WEAK POINTS:

*You must see
a competitor's
most serious
weak points
and focus your
strengths on
exploiting them.*

¹³The enemy has weak points.
Prepare your men against them.
He has strong points.
Make his men prepare themselves against you.

You must know the battleground. 6
You must know the time of battle.
You can then travel a thousand miles and still win the battle.

⁴The enemy should not know the battleground.
He shouldn't know the time of battle.
His left flank will be unable to support his right.
His right will be unable to support his left.
His front lines will be unable to support his rear.
His rear will be unable to support his front.
His support is distant even if it is only ten miles away.
What unknown place can be close?

¹²You control the balance of forces.
The enemy may have many men but they are superfluous.
How can they help him to victory?

If competitors focus on price, they sacrifice quality.
If they focus on quality, they are vulnerable on price.
If they focus on speed, they lose consistency.
If they focus on consistency, they lose speed.
Without knowing your focus, they cannot meet you directly.
If they claim every advantage, they are weak everywhere.

All markets have unmet needs.
Prepare your products to address those needs.
Competitors can satisfy some customers.
Encourage them to try to satisfy all possible customers.

NEEDS:

The marketplace has an infinite number of needs. You must choose those that you can best address.

6 You must choose what needs to address.
You must know where the marketplace is headed.
Then you can invest in product development and still make money.

Competitors must not identify the needs you target.
They must never know what market you are going after.
Competitors who market globally miss local markets.
If they market to everyone, they miss specialized needs.
If they sell to large companies, they ignore small customers.
If they sell to households, they overlook big opportunity.
They can miss your market, even if it is right in front of them.
If they do not understand your market, how can they fight you?

You decide the balance of power when you pick a target.
Competitors may be bigger, but they are not where you are.
How can their size hurt you?

[15]We say:
You must let victory happen.

[17]The enemy may have many men.
You can still control him without a fight.

When you form your strategy, know the strengths and
weaknesses of your plan.
When you execute a plan, know how to manage both action
and inaction.
When you take a position, know the deadly and the winning
grounds.
When you enter into battle, know when you have too many
or too few men.

[5]Use your position as your war's centerpiece.
Arrive at the battle without a formation.
Don't take a position in advance.
Then even the best spies can't report it.
Even the wisest general cannot plan to counter you.
Take a position where you can triumph using superior numbers.
Keep opposing forces ignorant.
Everyone should learn your location after your position has
given you success.
No one should know how your location gives you a winning
position.
Make a successful battle one from which the enemy cannot
recover.
You must continually adjust your position to his position.

We say:
Let the market make you successful.

Competitors may be much more powerful than you are.
You can still outmaneuver them by avoiding a confrontation.

7 When you create a marketing plan, know its strengths and weaknesses.
When you go after a target market, know which needs to satisfy and which to ignore.
When you position your product, know what areas are unprofitable and what is profitable.
When you are challenged, know when you have the advantage and when you are overmatched.

Look to leverage your existing markets to win new ones.
Go into new markets without an obvious aim.
Don't advertise what your goals are.
Your competitors cannot outmaneuver you.
You can beat good competitors if they do not know what to expect.
Go after segments in which you can become the dominant player.
Keep your competition in the dark.
Competitors should learn what your target market was only after you establish dominance.
Competitors should not know how you became so strong in any particular market niche.
Make sure that competitors cannot steal a market back from you once it is won.
To protect your market, mimic any moves competitors make.

Manage your military position like water. 8
Water takes every shape.
It avoids the high and moves to the low.
Your war can take any shape.
It must avoid the strong and strike the weak.
Water follows the shape of the land that directs its flow.
Your forces follow the enemy, who determines how you win.

[8]Make war without a standard approach.
Water has no consistent shape.
If you follow the enemy's shifts and changes, you can always
find a way to win.
We call this shadowing.

[12]Fight five different campaigns without a firm rule for victory.
Use all four seasons without a consistent position.
Your timing must be sudden.
A few weeks determine your failure or success.

ADJUSTMENT:

*Continuously
adjust to continu-
ous change.*

8 You must remain fluid in your product positioning.
Products can be positioned in many ways.
You start in a small niche and then expand.
You can adjust to different customer groups.
You must avoid competitors and address people's needs.
Profitability shapes your market and directs your products.
You discover your customers and let them determine your choices.

You must avoid rigid marketing plans.
Good ideas are always a little different.
You win markets by knowing your competitors' moves and adapting to the openings they leave.
Stay where they do not see you.

Change your approach, because no single message always wins.
Leverage the changing trends in the marketplace.
You must continually create a sense of urgency.
Focus on creating a continuous flow of dollars.

✦ ✦ ✦

URGENCY:

*Marketing must
focus on making
profits quickly.*

Related Articles from *Sun Tzu's Playbook*

In chapter six, Sun Tzu explains how to find opportunities by leveraging opposites. To learn the step-by-step techniques involved, we recommend the Sun Tzu's Art of War Playbook *articles listed below.*

1.2.1 Competitive Landscapes: the arenas in which rivals jockey for position.

1.2.2 Exploiting Exploration: how competitive landscapes are searched and positions utilized.

1.2.3 Position Complexity: how strategic positions arise from interactions in complex environments.

1.3.1 Competitive Comparison: competition as the comparison of positions.

2.4 Contact Networks: the range of contacts needed to create perspective.

2.4.1 Ground Perspective: getting information on a new competitive arena.

2.4.2 Climate Perspective: getting perspective on temporary external conditions.

2.4.3 Command Perspective: developing sources for understanding decision-makers.

2.4.4 Methods Perspective: developing contacts who understand best practices.

2.4.5 Mission Perspective: how we develop and use a perspective on motivation.

2.5 The Big Picture: building big-picture strategic awareness.

2.6 Knowledge Leverage: getting competitive value out of knowledge.

2.7 Information Secrecy: the role of limiting information in controlling relationships.

3.2.3 Complementary Opposites: the dynamics of balance from opposing forces.

3.2.4 Emptiness and Fullness: rules on the transformations between emptiness and fullness.

3.2.5 Dynamic Reversal: how situations reverse themselves naturally.

3.5 Strength and Weakness: six rules regarding openings created by the strength of others.

3.6 Leveraging Subjectivity: openings between subjective and objective positions.

3.7 Defining the Ground: redefining a competitive arena to create relative mismatches.

3.8 Strategic Matrix Analysis: two-dimensional representations of strategic space.

4.7 Competitive Weakness: how certain opportunities can bring out our weaknesses.

4.7.1 Command Weaknesses: the character flaws of leaders and how to exploit them.

4.7.2 Group Weaknesses: organizational weakness and where groups fail.

6.7 Tailoring to Conditions: overcoming opposition using conditions in the environment.

6.7.1 Form Adjustments: adapting responses based on the form of the ground.

6.7.2 Size Adjustments: adapting responses based on comparing size of forces.

6.7.3 Strength Adjustments: adapting responses based on unity of opposing forces.

6.8 Competitive Psychology: improving competitive psychology even in adversity and failure.

6.8.1 Adversity and Creativity: how we use adversity to spark our creativity.

6.8.2 Strength in Adversity: using adversity to increase a group's unity and focus.

Chapter 7

軍 爭

Armed Conflict — Communication

In the end, you must meet the competition in the marketplace. In modern marketing, this contact takes place through communications media. In the end, customers must make a choice between your product and those offered by your competitors. Classical strategy teaches that success depends less upon beating the competition in these situations than on how efficiently you build up your position so that when you do meet the competition, you have the advantage.

How do you build up a decisive advantage in communicating with your target market? Market communication is costly. If you rely simply upon spending more money than your competitors to develop a marketing edge, you are courting disaster. The secret is controlling the perceptions of both your potential customers and your competitors. Your customers and your competitors do not hear the same messages in the same way. You shape messages so that customers appreciate them but competitors disregard them.

All messages must be amplified. Just getting your message out isn't enough. It must attract attention and be simple to understand. You must make market contact at the proper time to take advantage of competitive weaknesses and motivate customers to act. Because market contact is the most important element in marketing, you must avoid a list of common potential mistakes discussed at the end of this chapter.

The Art of War: **Armed Conflict**

SUN TZU SAID:

Everyone uses the arts of war. **1**
You accept orders from the government.
Then you assemble your army.
You organize your men and build camps.
You must avoid disasters from armed conflict.

⁶Seeking armed conflict can be disastrous.
Because of this, a detour can be the shortest path.
Because of this, problems can become opportunities.

⁹Use an indirect route as your highway.
Use the search for advantage to guide you.
When you fall behind, you must catch up.
When you get ahead, you must wait.
You must know the detour that most directly
accomplishes your plan.

¹⁴Undertake armed conflict when you have an
advantage.
Seeking armed conflict for its own sake is dangerous.

CONFLICT:

Strategy teaches
that conflict is
always costly
so it is ideally
avoided when-
ever possible.

The Art of Marketing: Communication

1 Everyone thinks they have a marketing strategy.
You get your direction from your organization.
You then put together your products.
You organize a campaign and develop your brand.
You must then avoid mistakes in communicating to the market.

Market communication is costly and tricky.
You must find a message everyone else is overlooking.
You must find the opportunity hidden in problems.

You can find unique channels of communication.
Let your quest for customers guide you.
If you have too few contacts, you must build them up.
If you get ahead of the market, you must wait for it.
You must find new avenues that take you directly to
your customers.

Only make marketing contact when you are ready to
sell.
Marketing communication for its own sake is dangerous.

CHANNELS:

*You must
manage your
communication
through both the
media and cus-
tomer relation-
ships.*

You can build up an army to fight for an advantage. 2
Then you won't catch the enemy.
You can force your army to go fight for an advantage.
Then you abandon your heavy supply wagons.

⁵You keep only your armor and hurry after the enemy.
You avoid stopping day or night.
You use many roads at the same time.
You go hundreds of miles to fight for an advantage.
Then the enemy catches your commanders and your army.
Your strong soldiers get there first.
Your weaker soldiers follow behind.
Using this approach, only one in ten will arrive.
You can try to go fifty miles to fight for an advantage.
Then your commanders and army will stumble.
Using this method, only half of your soldiers will make it.
You can try to go thirty miles to fight for an advantage.
Then only two out of three get there.

¹⁸If you make your army travel without good
supply lines, your army will die.
Without supplies and food, your army will die.
If you don't save the harvest, your army will die.

FIGHTING:

You do not create opportunities by fighting for them. The use of force without strategy is wasted effort.

2 You can build communication based upon only advertising.
You will then fall behind your competitors.
You can throw away any amount of money to send your message.
But you then sacrifice the creation of communication channels.

You can be confident and rush into an advertising program.
You can advertise day and night.
You can advertise in every medium available.
You can advertise to get your product known everywhere.
Then competing products will take away your customers and sales.
Your message will get out there.
Your ability to deliver products and satisfaction will lag behind.
Only a small fraction of your efforts will result in good business.
You can advertise in hopes of building a communication system.
This only results in problems running your company.
By relying on advertising, you make sales but not profits.
You limit your budget for advertising communication.
Then your sales will be marginally profitable.

If you go to market without creating communication
channels, your organization will fail.
Without money and resources, organizations fail.
Without profitable repeat business, organizations fail.

ADVERTISING:

Advertising is tricky. Mostly it is a form of force used by those with more money than wisdom.

21Do not let any of your potential enemies know what you are planning.
Still, you must not hesitate to form alliances.
You must know the mountains and forests.
You must know where the obstructions are.
You must know where the marshes are.
If you don't, you cannot move the army.
If you don't, you must use local guides.
If you don't, you can't take advantage of the terrain.

You make war using a deceptive position. 3
If you use deception, then you can move.
Using deception, you can upset the enemy and change the situation.
You can move as quickly as the wind.
You can rise like the forest.
You can invade and plunder like fire.
You can stay as motionless as a mountain.
You can be as mysterious as the fog.
You can strike like sounding thunder.

DECEPTION:

Success comes from controlling people's perceptions by shaping the way situations must appear to them.

10Divide your troops to plunder the villages.
When on open ground, dividing is an advantage.
Don't worry about organization; just move.
Be the first to find a new route that leads directly to a winning plan.
This is how you are successful at armed conflict.

Good communication channels start with working below the competition's radar.
You must create partnerships, distributors, and supporters.
You must know your market and your customers.
You must know where the potential problems are.
You must avoid getting bogged down in logistics.
If you do not, you cannot move your products.
You must create relationships in the marketplace.
If you do not, you will not win in your market.

3 You must make selling look like information and entertainment.
Using public relations, you can advance your position.
Use the free media coverage gained through public relations to make competitors look bad by comparison.
Publicity programs can get your message out quickly.
Publicity programs magnify you.
You can use media coverage to get customers to buy now.
You can avoid unwanted attention.
You can create a sense of mystery and possibility.
You can get your message out everywhere.

Use all types of publicity to sell to broad markets.
Since the media is wide open, spreading out works.
Do not be selective; just get your message out.
Being the first to discover a new publicity hook creates a winning campaign.
This is how you are successful at communication.

PUBLICITY:

You cannot appear to sell when getting publicity, but this makes it the most powerful selling tool.

Military experience says: 4
"You can speak, but you will not be heard.
You must use gongs and drums.
You cannot really see your forces just by looking.
You must use banners and flags."

[6]You must master gongs, drums, banners, and flags.
Place people as a single unit where they can all see and hear.
You must unite them as one.
Then the brave cannot advance alone.
The fearful cannot withdraw alone.
You must force them to act as a group.

[12]In night battles, you must use numerous fires and drums.
In day battles, you must use many banners and flags.
You must position your people to control what they see and
hear.

You control your army by controlling its morale. 5
As a general, you must be able to control emotions.

[3]In the morning, a person's energy is high.
During the day, it fades.
By evening, a person's thoughts turn to home.
You must use your troops wisely.
Avoid the enemy's high spirits.
Strike when his men are lazy and want to go home.
This is how you master energy.

4 Experience in marketing teaches us this:
"You can communicate, but you will not be heard.
You must be inventive to get people's attention.
You cannot be seen just by having a presence.
You must use showmanship and drama."

Use gimmicks and tricks to get the market's attention.
Communicate in a way that reaches your entire market.
Tie your campaign's themes together.
Do not put forth novel ideas alone.
Tie them with comfortable, familiar concepts.
Every campaign must amplify a single, clear message.

When you are unknown, you must create excitement.
If you are better known, you must still be interesting.
You must use communication that allows target customers to see
and appreciate what you offer.

5 You make communication work by generating emotion.
You must also be able to control your own emotions.

At the start of a communication campaign, sales resistance is high.
As people become familiar with you, resistance fades.
When it is time to buy, people want safety and security.
You must time your messages correctly.
Avoid creating market resistance.
Win customers when resistance fades and buyers want security.
You must maintain the energy in communication.

¹⁰Use discipline to await the chaos of battle.
Keep relaxed to await a crisis.
This is how you master emotion.

¹³Stay close to home to await a distant enemy.
Stay comfortable to await the weary enemy.
Stay well fed to await the hungry enemy.
This is how you master power.

Don't entice the enemy when his ranks are orderly. 6
You must not attack when his formations are solid.
This is how you master adaptation.

⁴You must follow these military rules.
Do not take a position facing the high ground.
Do not oppose those with their backs to the wall.
Do not follow those who pretend to flee.
Do not attack the enemy's strongest men.
Do not swallow the enemy's bait.
Do not block an army that is heading home.
Leave an escape outlet for a surrounded army.
Do not press a desperate foe.
This is how you use military skills.

EMOTION:

Strategy teaches that emotion is the key to action. If you control emotions, you control actions.

† † †

You must stay on message when you communicate.
Keep calm when you are inevitably challenged.
You must control your own emotions.

Stake your claim and wait for customers to come to you.
Stay positive and wait for skepticism to fade.
Stay profitable and wait for customers to feel their needs.
Patience is how communication gives you power.

6 Do not talk to markets about what is going well.
Do not challenge people where they do not feel a need.
You must adapt to their needs.

You must follow these communication rules:
Do not take a marketing position against what is right and true.
Do not take away people's choices.
Do not attack those that you think are weak.
Do not confront your competitors' strongest messages.
Do not believe everything that the market tells you.
Do not make it difficult for customers to buy.
Give people easy choices to make.
Do not make customers feel pressured.
These are the rules of market communication.

✦ ✦ ✦

MESSAGE:

Your message must not be how great you or your products are, but how you can make your customers great.

Related Articles from *Sun Tzu's Playbook*

In chapter seven, Sun Tzu teaches us to focus on building positions instead of on tearing down opponents. To learn the step-by-step techniques involved, we recommend the Sun Tzu's Art of War Playbook *articles listed below.*

1.2.1 Competitive Landscapes: the arenas in which rivals jockey for position.

1.3.1 Competitive Comparison: competition as the comparison of positions.

1.5 Competing Agents: characteristics of competitors.

1.7 Competitive Power: the sources of superiority in challenges.

1.8.1 Creation and Destruction: the creation and destruction of competitive positions.

1.9 Competition and Production: the two opposing skill sets of competition and production.

2.1.3 Strategic Deception: misinformation and disinformation in competition.

2.6 Knowledge Leverage: getting competitive value out of knowledge.

2.7 Information Secrecy: the role of secrecy in relationships.

3.1 Strategic Economics: balancing the cost and benefits of positioning.

3.1.1 Resource Limitations: the inherent limitation of strategic resources.

3.1.3 Conflict Cost: the costly nature of resolving competitive comparisons by conflict.

3.1.6 Time Limitations: understanding the time limits on opportunities.

3.7 Defining the Ground: redefining a competitive arena to create relative mismatches.

4.7 Competitive Weakness: how certain opportunities can bring out our weaknesses.

6.1.2 Prioritizing Conditions: parsing complex competitive conditions into simple responses.

6.8 Competitive Psychology: improving competitive psychology even in adversity and failure.

7.4 Competitive Timing: the role of timing in creating momentum.

7.6 Productive Competition: using momentum to produce more resources.

7.6.2 Ground Creation: the creation of new competitive ground to be successful.

8.5 Leveraging Emotions: how we use emotion to obtain rewards.

9.5.2 Avoiding Emotion: the danger of exploiting environmental vulnerabilities for purely emotion reasons.

Chapter 8

九變

Adaptability – Resilience

Warrior marketing is not a plan. In many ways the science of strategy is the opposite of planning. Strategy is a process that continually adjusts plans based upon changing conditions. Since markets change not only from year to year but from day to day, successful marketing strategies must be dynamic.

This chapter serves as a short introduction to the next three long chapters that explain a variety of specific strategic situations. The message is that strategy requires that you correctly diagnose your situations and respond appropriately. This chapter starts with a list of specific situations that are covered in greater detail in the following chapters. All these situations require adjustments to your plans.

By preparing yourself to adapt to circumstances, you create resilience. You can creatively respond to your situation. You naturally begin to look for ways to use the dynamics of a changing situation to leverage your position. You begin to see every change not as a blessing or a curse, but as a challenge to be explored.

Warrior marketing addresses the unpredictable nature of other people in planning the defense of your market position. The biggest danger in strategy is failing to prepare yourself mentally for what might go wrong. The chapter ends by listing five weaknesses of people and explains how easily these weaknesses can be exploited in the dynamics of competition.

The Art of War: **Adaptability**

Everyone uses the arts of war. 1
As a general, you get your orders from the government.
You gather your troops.
On dangerous ground, you must not camp.
Where the roads intersect, you must join your allies.
When an area is cut off, you must not delay in it.
When you are surrounded, you must scheme.
In a life-or-death situation, you must fight.
There are roads that you must not take.
There are armies that you must not fight.
There are strongholds that you must not attack.
There are positions that you must not defend.
There are government commands that must not be
obeyed.

ADAPTABILITY:

Adaptability doesn't mean doing what you want. It means knowing the appropriate response to the situation.

[14]Military leaders must be experts in knowing how
to adapt to find an advantage.
This will teach you the use of war.

The Art of Marketing: Resilience

A MARKETING WARRIOR HEARS:

1 Everyone is out there putting together their marketing plans.
In marketing, you get your direction from your organization.
Then you gather your resources.
Where you find market conditions are bad, you must move on.
Where alliances are needed, you must find partners.
When a market offers no future, you avoid it.
When competitors are all around, you get creative.
When you are in a do-or-die situation, you challenge competitors.
There are communication channels that you must avoid.
There are market segments that you do not want.
There are competitors that you cannot challenge.
There are product positions that you cannot defend.
Some organizations are wrong about what they think they want.

Warrior marketing means adapting to market situations and finding opportunities in them.
Adapting to market situations is the key to success.

RESILIENCE:

You become more resilient when you see that no situation is good or bad in itself. All that matters is your response.

[16]Some commanders are not good at making adjustments to find an advantage.
They can know the shape of the terrain.
Still, they cannot find an advantageous position.

[19]Some military commanders do not know how to adjust their methods.
They can find an advantageous position.
Still, they cannot use their men effectively.

You must be creative in your planning. 2
You must adapt to your opportunities and weaknesses.
You can use a variety of approaches and still have a consistent result.
You must adjust to a variety of problems and consistently solve them.

You can deter your potential enemy by using his 3
weaknesses against him.
You can keep your potential enemy's army busy by giving it work to do.
You can rush your potential enemy by offering him an advantageous position.

PLANNING:

Planning does not mean creating a rigid to-do list, but constantly rethinking what the situation demands.

Some marketing people are unable to change their approach to take advantage of an opportunity.

They can see the opportunity in the market.

They cannot see how to use it to advance their market position.

Some marketing people are unable to change their methods to fit market conditions.

They can figure out what the right position is.

They are unable to change their system to take advantage of it.

2 You must be inventive in developing your marketing responses.

You must change what you are doing when the market changes.

You must adjust your methods to create consistency in a fast-changing market.

Every market situation offers unique difficulties, but you can learn to find good market responses.

3 In every changing situation, you must think about the problems your competitors have.

You must challenge your competitors to respond to changes as you do.

Every change in the marketplace creates the potential for rushing competitors into making mistakes.

CHANGE:

Marketing warriors embrace change so that they can respond more quickly than their competitors.

You must make use of war. 4
Do not trust that the enemy isn't coming.
Trust your readiness to meet him.
Do not trust that the enemy won't attack.
Rely only on your ability to pick a place that the enemy can't attack.

You can exploit five different faults in a leader. 5
If he is willing to die, you can kill him.
If he wants to survive, you can capture him.
He may have a quick temper.
You can then provoke him with insults.
If he has a delicate sense of honor, you can disgrace him.
If he loves his people, you can create problems for him.
In every situation, look for these five weaknesses.
They are common faults in commanders.
They always lead to military disaster.

[11]To overturn an army, you must kill its general.
To do this, you must use these five weaknesses.
You must always look for them.

PREPARATION:

The battlefield always favors those who are the most mentally prepared for things not going according to plan.

4 You must use competitive pressure.
Do not expect to win any market without resistance.
Instead, be resourceful in meeting resistance.
Do not trust that competitors will not come after your customers.
Instead, position and brand your products so that others cannot easily attack them.

5 Changing market conditions can expose real weaknesses.
If you are willing to lose customers, you will lose them.
If you lack courage, you can be scared out of markets.
Perhaps you tend to overreact.
Market pressure then provokes you into making mistakes.
If you are sensitive to criticism, surprises can embarrass you.
If you grow attached to things as they are, change is a barrier.
In a changing situation, watch for these five weaknesses.
They commonly lead to mistakes in marketing.
They can lead you to market disaster.

These weaknesses can destroy you and your campaign.
You must know how to exploit them in competitors.
You must always be aware of them.

✦ ✦ ✦

FLAWS:

People naturally resist change, but you can prepare yourself to resist making the mistakes you are the most prone to.

Related Articles from *Sun Tzu's Playbook*

In chapter eight, Sun Tzu teaches us the need to constantly adapt to the situation. To learn the step-by-step techniques involved, we recommend the Sun Tzu's Art of War Playbook *articles listed below.*

1.8 Progress Cycle: the adaptive loop by which positions are advanced.

1.8.1 Creation and Destruction : the creation and destruction of competitive positions.

1.8.2 The Adaptive Loop: the continual reiteration of position analysis.

1.8.3 Cycle Time: the importance of speed in feedback and reaction.

1.8.4 Probabilistic Process: the role of chance in strategic processes and systems.

4.7.1 Command Weaknesses: the character flaws of leaders and how to exploit them.

5.2.1 Choosing Adaptability: choosing actions that allow us a maximum of future flexibility.

5.2.2 Campaign Methods: the use of campaigns and their methods.

5.2.3 Unplanned Steps: distinguishing campaign adjustments from steps in a plan.

5.3 Reaction Time: the use of speed in choosing actions.

5.3.1 Speed and Quickness: the use of pace within a dynamic environment.

6.0 Situation Response: selecting the actions most appropriate to a situation.

6.1 Situation Recognition: situation recognition in making advances.

6.1.1 Conditioned Reflexes: how we develop automatic, instantaneous responses.

6.1.2 Prioritizing Conditions: parsing complex competitive conditions into simple responses.

6.2 Campaign Evaluation: how we justify continued investment in an ongoing campaign.

6.2.1 Campaign Flow: seeing campaigns as a series of situations that flow logically from one to another.

6.2.2 Campaign Goals: assessing the value of a campaign by a larger mission.

6.3 Campaign Patterns: how knowing campaign stages gives us insight into our situation.

6.5 Nine Responses: the best responses to the nine common competitive situations.

6.7 Tailoring to Conditions: overcoming opposition using conditions in the environment.

6.7.1 Form Adjustments: adapting our responses based on the form of the ground.

6.7.2 Size Adjustments: adapting responses based on the relative size of opposing forces.

6.7.3 Strength Adjustments: how to adapt responses based on the relative strength of opposing missions.

Chapter 9

行軍

Armed March — Campaigns

This long chapter addresses the challenges encountered in adjusting a campaign to changing market conditions. The last chapter discussed the general need for adaptability. In this chapter, we examine specific types of market conditions and how a marketing warrior adapts to them. Strategy demands that you both recognize the situation and know how to respond to it.

Marketing campaigns take place in four different types of general market environments—difficult, fluid, uncertain, or broad. When your campaign runs into these conditions, you must know the right way to respond.

Campaigns must balance the question of value. Warrior strategy dictates that over the long term, it is better to market on the basis of superior quality than the lowest prices. It is often easier to campaign on price, but this weak position creates problems over time.

There are seasonal and hidden dangers inherent in any marketing campaign. Strategy dictates that you must analyze competitors' words and actions to know how to respond. Since competitors don't tell you what they are doing, you must determine the conditions and intentions of your opponents by interpreting their behavior and that of their employees.

When has a campaign gone far enough? How do you respond when you see these signs? Campaigns have to pause when the resources you need to make sales are stretched too thin. You must then stop and train new people, especially new sales channels.

The Art of War: **Armed March**

SUN TZU SAID:

Anyone moving an army must adjust to the enemy. 1
When caught in the mountains, rely on their valleys.
Position yourself on the heights facing the sun.
To win your battles, never attack uphill.
This is how you position your army in the mountains.

6When water blocks you, keep far away from it.
Let the invader cross the river and wait for him.
Do not meet him in midstream.
Wait for him to get half his forces across and then
take advantage of the situation.

10You need to be able to fight.
You can't do that if you are caught in water when
you meet an invader.
Position yourself upstream, facing the sun.
Never face against the current.
Always position your army upstream when near
the water.

TERRAIN:

*Strategy teaches
that all terrains
have a different
form and these
forms dictate
how you must
respond.*

The Art of Marketing: Campaigns

A MARKETING WARRIOR HEARS:

1 In any marketing campaign, you adjust to your customers.
When markets get difficult, keep to the easiest customers.
Seek a visible presence as a market leader.
To win the market, never attack the market leader.
This is how you campaign in difficult markets.

When a frenzy affects your industry, avoid it.
Let your competitors get involved in passing fads.
Do not battle competitors over the latest short-lived trend.
Wait for competitors to get caught up in the mania, and
then take advantage of them.

You need to stay competitive.
You cannot accurately predict future sales when trying
to compete on the latest fashion.
Visibly position yourself with the long-term trends.
Never fight against any trends.
Always take advantage of long-term trends when
positioning your products.

MARKETS:

*Markets have
different forms
just like terrains
do. They can be
difficult, fluid,
uncertain, or
just broad.*

15You may have to move across marshes.
Move through them quickly without stopping.
You may meet the enemy in the middle of a marsh.
You must keep on the water grasses.
Keep your back to a clump of trees.
This is how you position your army in a marsh.

21On a level plateau, take a position that you can change.
Keep the higher ground on your right and to the rear.
Keep danger in front of you and safety behind.
This is how you position yourself on a level plateau.

25You can find an advantage in all four of these situations.
Learn from the great emperor who used positioning to
conquer his four rivals.

Armies are stronger on high ground and weaker on low. 2
They are better camping on sunny southern hillsides than
on shady northern ones.
Provide for your army's health and place men correctly.
Your army will be free from disease.
Done correctly, this means victory.

6You must sometimes defend on a hill or riverbank.
You must keep on the south side in the sun.
Keep the uphill slope at your right rear.

9This will give the advantage to your army.
It will always give you a position of strength.

You may discover that your target market is unstable.
Get through that market quickly and move to a more stable one.
You get into market battles during market uncertainty.
If you do, keep to the most dependable parts of the market.
Do whatever you can to prevent surprises.
This is how you campaign in an uncertain market.

In broad markets, keep your positioning flexible.
Offer a high-quality product and get attention.
Stay in front of the competition and avoid missteps.
This is how you campaign in broad markets.

You can find an advantage in any market.
Study the successes of those who have done well in each of these
types of markets.

2 Marketing is better when selling quality rather than price.
You are better off staking out a highly visible, quality position than
a bargain one.
Keep your market position strong by giving it a quality image.
Your organization must be proud of its products.
Doing this correctly will win you markets.

Sometimes you must defend a higher price.
Make the better value of your product known.
You always want to offer the best value for the price.

Quality will always give an advantage to your campaign.
It will always give you a position of strength.

Stop the march when the rain swells the river into rapids. 3
You may want to ford the river.
Wait until it subsides.

4All regions can have seasonal mountain streams that can
cut you off.
There are seasonal lakes.
There are seasonal blockages.
There are seasonal jungles.
There are seasonal floods.
There are seasonal fissures.
Get away from all these quickly.
Do not get close to them.
Keep them at a distance.
Maneuver the enemy close to them.
Position yourself facing these dangers.
Push the enemy back into them.

16Danger can hide on your army's flank.
There are reservoirs and lakes.
There are reeds and thickets.
There are mountain woods.
Their dense vegetation provides a hiding place.
You must cautiously search through them.
They can always hide an ambush.

SEASONS:

*The changing
climate part of
every strategic
position means
that positions
continually
change.*

3 Stop your campaign when your target market is in turmoil.
You may want to use the press.
Wait until the furor subsides.

All marketplaces suffer temporary conditions that can hurt marketing campaigns.
There are overstocks.
There are shortages.
There are mix-ups.
There are surpluses.
There are bankruptcies.
Avoid the problem areas in markets.
Do not rely on risky customers.
Minimize your involvement with potential problems.
Let your competition struggle with them.
Keep your eye on these difficulties.
Let your competitors be surprised by them.

Hidden risks can endanger your campaign.
Fashion can become fad.
Variety can become confusion.
The difficult can become impossible.
The confusion of markets can always surprise you.
You must continually analyze your market.
You do not want to be surprised.

PATIENCE:

Market changes endanger campaigns only if you rush into them without realizing what is happening.

Sometimes, the enemy is close by but remains calm. 4
Expect to find him in a natural stronghold.
Other times he remains at a distance but provokes battle.
He wants you to attack him.

5He sometimes shifts the position of his camp.
He is looking for an advantageous position.

7The trees in the forest move.
Expect that the enemy is coming.
The tall grasses obstruct your view.
Be suspicious.

COMPETITION:

Competition is part of the competitive environment and must be analyzed as part of that environment.

11The birds take flight.
Expect that the enemy is hiding.
Animals startle.
Expect an ambush.

15Notice the dust.
It sometimes rises high in a straight line.
Vehicles are coming.
The dust appears low in a wide band.
Foot soldiers are coming.
The dust seems scattered in different areas.
The enemy is collecting firewood.
Any dust is light and settling down.
The enemy is setting up camp.

4 Competitors sell to your marketplace but they are quiet.
You should expect that they have a solid position.
Competitors distance their products from yours.
They plan to threaten your product position.

A competitor's product position seems to invite attack.
Always expect that your opponent has a secret advantage.

Opinions in the market begin to change.
Expect that a competitor is active.
The market is difficult to evaluate.
Expect to be surprised once you are in it.

Market observers are suddenly quiet.
Suspect that a competitor is sharing a secret.
Buyers suddenly stop buying.
A competitor is undercutting you.

EVALUATION:

Competitors don't tell you what they are planning, so you must judge them by what you see in the market.

Ask for information about competitors.
News can come from market leaders and consultants.
Expect a quick, direct marketing campaign against you.
News can come from everywhere in the market.
This means that competitors have many salespeople active.
News of competitors is scattered in different areas.
This means that they are researching the market.
News of competitors becomes rarer and rarer.
This means that they are waiting.

Your enemy speaks humbly while building up forces. 5
He is planning to advance.

³The enemy talks aggressively and pushes as if to advance.
He is planning to retreat.

⁵Small vehicles exit his camp first.
They move the army's flanks.
They are forming a battle line.

⁸Your enemy tries to sue for peace but without offering a treaty.
He is plotting.

¹⁰Your enemy's men run to leave and yet form ranks.
You should expect action.

¹²Half his army advances and the other half retreats.
He is luring you.

¹⁴Your enemy plans to fight but his men just stand there.
They are starving.

¹⁶Those who draw water drink it first.
They are thirsty.

¹⁸Your enemy sees an advantage but does not advance.
His men are tired.

5 A competitor denies interest in your market but is researching it.
Prepare for a full campaign.

Competitors say they want a market but do not campaign.
Expect them to give up.

Competitors advertise in your market.
They support advertising with a sales effort.
They are serious about winning your customers.

Competitors want to discuss an agreement but without making a
real contract.
Expect them to mislead you.

Competitors withdraw but reorganize their sales force.
Expect them to come back again.

Some competitors leave a market while others go after it.
Do not be lured into that market.

A competitor truly targets a market, but is idle.
The organization is out of resources.

A competitor offers incentives for paying cash.
The company is short of money.

Competitors have more opportunity but don't take advantage of it.
They are too busy to do more.

²⁰Birds gather.
Your enemy has abandoned his camp.

²²Your enemy's soldiers call in the night.
They are afraid.

²⁴Your enemy's army is raucous.
The men do not take their commander seriously.

²⁶Your enemy's banners and flags shift.
Order is breaking down.

²⁸Your enemy's officers are irritable.
They are exhausted.

JUDGMENT:

You best judge your competitors' situation by what they and their employees do rather than what they say.

³⁰Your enemy's men kill their horses for meat.
They are out of provisions.

³²They don't put their pots away or return to their
tents.
They are desperate.

³⁴Enemy troops appear sincere and agreeable.
But their men are slow to speak to each other.
They are no longer united.

³⁷Your enemy offers too many incentives to his men.
He is in trouble.

Consultants come to you.
Your competitor has abandoned the marketplace.

Competitors' employees make contact with you.
They are worried.

A competitor's employees expose problems.
They do not take their company's management seriously.

A competitor suddenly changes its message and image.
The company is falling apart.

A competitor's top managers are easily angered.
They are stretched thin.

A competitor suspends advertising.
The company is short of funds.

A competitor sacrifices resources and closes down
offices.
The management has no choice.

A competitor's allies seem friendly with each other.
Nevertheless, they are slow to communicate.
Their alliances are failing.

A competitor offers too many incentives to buy.
The company is not making sales goals.

Problems:

In market competition, you need to take advantage of the problems that your competitors are having.

[39]Your enemy gives out too many punishments.
His men are weary.

[41]Your enemy first acts violently and then is afraid of your
larger force.
His best troops have not arrived.

[43]Your enemy comes in a conciliatory manner.
He needs to rest and recuperate.

[45]Your enemy is angry and appears to welcome battle.
This goes on for a long time, but he doesn't attack.
He also doesn't leave the field.
You must watch him carefully.

If you are too weak to fight, you must find more men. 6
In this situation, you must not act aggressively.
You must unite your forces.
Prepare for the enemy.
Recruit men and stay where you are.

[6]You must be cautious about making plans and
adjust to the enemy.
You must gather more men.

EXPANSION:

*Campaigns
into new areas
expand your
control but they
also spread your
resources over a
wider territory.*

Competitors make it more difficult to buy.
Their people have many bad accounts.

A competitor wins customers and then quickly withdraws from
your market.
The company needs to develop more resources.

A competitor suggests partnering with you.
Their organization is simply buying time.

A competitor sounds aggressive but does not campaign.
The company remains in the market without attacking you.
It does not withdraw from the market either.
You must keep your eye on this company.

6 When a campaign runs thin on resources, you rebuild them.
You must not campaign aggressively when you are stretched thin.
You must consolidate your markets.
You must defend what you have won.
You must build up resources and take a break.

You must adjust to your changing situation rather
than sticking to the plans you've made.
You need resources to continue growing.

PAUSING:

*A marketing
campaign reach-
es its limit when
your resources
are stretched
too thin to make
more sales.*

With new, undedicated soldiers, you can depend on them 7
if you discipline them.
They will tend to disobey your orders.
If they do not obey your orders, they will be useless.

4You can depend on seasoned, dedicated soldiers.
But you must avoid disciplining them without reason.
Otherwise, you cannot use them.

7You must control your soldiers with esprit de corps.
You must bring them together by winning victories.
You must get them to believe in you.

10Make it easy for people to know what to do by training
your people.
Your people will then obey you.
If you do not make it easy for people to know what
to do, you won't train your people.
Then they will not obey.

14Make your commands easy to follow.
You must understand the way a crowd thinks.

YOUR TROOPS:

*Your success
depends totally
on your ability to
train, motivate,
and manage
the people with
whom you work.*

7 With new sales channels, you must be consistent with your marketing programs.
Otherwise, salespeople will get confused.
If they are confused, they cannot help you.

It is different with established sales channels.
You must show flexibility.
They serve you best by giving you new ideas.

You control your sales channels through sharing your success.
You must win them over by generating sales through them.
They must believe that you are valuable.

Make it easy for salespeople to sell your product by educating them about benefits.
They will then follow your direction.
If you make your offering too complex, you will not be able to train people to sell it.
They will stop listening to you.

You must make your offering easy to understand.
You must understand how groups of people think.

♦ ♦ ♦

SALES:

Campaigns must include training and managing sales channels if you are going to generate revenue.

Related Articles from *Sun Tzu's Playbook*

In chapter nine, Sun Tzu discusses the basics of recognizing conditions in new territory. To learn the step-by-step techniques involved, we recommend the Sun Tzu's Art of War Playbook *articles listed below.*

1.1.0 Position Paths: the continuity of strategic positions over time.

1.2.2 Exploiting Exploration: how competitive landscapes are searched and positions utilized.

2.1 Information Value: knowledge and communication as the basis of strategy.

2.1.1 Information Limits: making good decisions with limited information.

2.2.1 Personal Relationships: why information depends on personal relationships.

2.2.2 Mental Models: how mental models simplify decision-making.

2.2.3 Standard Terminology: how mental models must be shared to enable communication.

2.3 Personal Interactions: making progress through personal interactions.

2.3.1 Action and Reaction: how we advance based on how others react to our actions.

2.3.2 Reaction Unpredictability: why we can never exactly predict the reactions of others.

2.3.3 Likely Reactions: the range of potential reactions in gathering information.

2.3.4 Using Questions: using questions in gathering information and predicting reactions.

4.0 Leveraging Probability: making better decisions regarding our choice of opportunities.

4.3 Leveraging Form: how we can leverage the form of our territory.

4.3.1 Tilted Forms: opportunities that are dominated by uneven forces.

4.3.2 Fluid Forms: opportunities that are dominated by fast-changing directional forces.

4.3.3 Soft Forms: opportunities that are dominated by forces that create uncertainty.

4.3.4 Neutral Forms: opportunities where the terrain has no dominant forces.

4.4 Strategic Distance: relative proximity in strategic space.

4.4.1 Physical Distance: the issues of proximity in physical space.

4.4.2 Intellectual Distance: the challenges of moving through intellectual space.

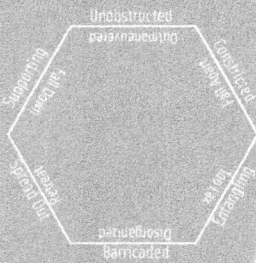

Chapter 10

地 形

Field Position – Opportunities

As your campaign moves into a new market, you learn a lot more about the opportunities that it offers. The strategy of warrior marketing isn't just concerned with the initial opportunity but with where that opportunity takes you. Strategically, each market position is simply a stepping-stone to a new position. Your concern is never where you have been but where you are going.

As you advance your market position, you must constantly reevaluate your situation and its future potential. You can target a market, but you only begin to learn its true nature once you are actually selling in it. Warrior marketing teaches that there are six typical types of market opportunities and that you must respond differently to each of them.

Your ability to deal with a specific type of opportunity depends on the nature of your campaign. These six different flaws in organizations arise in and are amplified by the specific type of market opportunity. If you know the type of campaign and the type of opportunity, you can avoid certain types of problems.

In warrior marketing, no position is permanent. Each is a stepping-stone to a new position. You must know the secret of making these transitions, especially the proper way of providing leadership to your people as you move into different situations.

The nature of the opportunity determines not only your response, but the position of your competitors. You must compare your different opportunities before choosing a course of action.

The Art of War: **Field Position**

SUN TZU SAID:

Some field positions are unobstructed. 1
Some field positions are entangling.
Some field positions are supporting.
Some field positions are constricted.
Some field positions give you a barricade.
Some field positions are spread out.

7You can attack from some positions easily.
Other forces can meet you easily as well.
We call these unobstructed positions.
These positions are open.
On them, be the first to occupy a high, sunny area.
Put yourself where you can defend your supply routes.
Then you will have an advantage.

IN THE FIELD:

*Strategy teaches
that you can
learn the true
nature of a
territory only
once you have
entered into it.*

The Art of Marketing: **Opportunities**

A MARKETING WARRIOR HEARS:

1 Some market opportunities are unrestricted.
Some market opportunities are tricky.
Some market opportunities are peaks.
Some market opportunities are exclusive.
Some market opportunities are easy to protect.
Some market opportunities are too dispersed.

You can campaign easily in some market segments.
Others can get into these markets easily as well.
These are unrestricted market opportunities.
These market segments offer no barriers to entry.
In these markets, seek well-publicized positions.
Concentrate on creating defensible channels.
This is the opportunity in unrestricted markets.

OPPORTUNITY:

There are six different forms of market opportunities and each requires the appropriate approach.

[14]You can attack from some positions easily.
Disaster arises when you try to return to them.
These are entangling positions.
These field positions are one-sided.
Wait until your enemy is unprepared.
You can then attack from these positions and win.
Avoid a well-prepared enemy.
You will try to attack and lose.
Since you can't return, you will meet disaster.
These field positions offer no advantage.

[24]You cannot leave some positions without losing an advantage.
If the enemy leaves this ground, he also loses an advantage.
We call these supporting field positions.
These positions strengthen you.
The enemy may try to entice you away.
Still, hold your position.
You must entice the enemy to leave.
You then strike him as he is leaving.
These field positions offer an advantage.

[33]Some field positions are constricted.
Get to these positions first.
You must fill these areas and await the enemy.
Sometimes, the enemy will reach them first.
If he fills them, do not follow him.
However, if he fails to fill them, you can go after him.

You can move out of some markets easily.
You cannot get back into them after leaving them.
These are tricky opportunities.
They give you one chance.
Wait for the right time to move on from them to new markets.
You can then move from tricky markets to win better ones.
Avoid moving from tricky markets into uncertain markets.
You can launch your campaign and it could fail.
Since you cannot go back to your old position, you are in trouble.
Tricky market opportunities offer no long-term advantage.

You cannot move away from some market opportunities without going downhill.
No one can improve on these market positions.
These are peak market opportunities.
They are the strongest possible positions in that market.
A competitor may try to lure you away from them.
You must hold your position.
If competitors are in a peak position, try to lure them away.
You can then take advantage of their poor decisions.
Do not take peak opportunities for granted.

Some market opportunities are exclusive.
You must establish these positions before competitors do.
You must satisfy the market and await competitors.
Competitors may establish themselves in these positions first.
If they satisfy the market, do not try to copy them.
If they leave openings, you can go after them.

³⁹Some field positions give you a barricade.
Get to these positions first.
You must occupy their southern, sunny heights in order to
await the enemy.
Sometimes the enemy occupies these areas first.
If so, entice him away.
Never go after him.

⁴⁵Some field positions are too spread out.
Your force may seem equal to the enemy.
Still you will lose if you provoke a battle.
If you fight, you will not have any advantage.

⁴⁹These are the six types of field positions.
Each battleground has its own rules.
As a commander, you must know where to go.
You must examine each position closely.

Some armies can be outmaneuvered. 2
Some armies are too lax.
Some armies fall down.
Some armies fall apart.
Some armies are disorganized.
Some armies must retreat.

YOUR FORCES:

*The term
"forces" means
all elements
used against the
competition,
both personnel
and resources.*

⁷Know all six of these weaknesses.
They create weak timing and disastrous positions.
They all arise from the army's commander.

Some market opportunities are easy to protect.
You must establish yourself in these markets before competitors do.
You then must aggressively publicize your position and await competitive attacks.
Sometimes competitors win these segments first.
If so, try to get competitors to abandon them.
Do not go after competitors in these positions.

Some market opportunities are too dispersed.
Your resources are too thinly spread-out to be competitive.
You are wasting your time on these opportunities.
They are too big for you to hold from a competitive challenge.

Know all six types of market opportunities.
Each market situation has its own rules.
In marketing, you must know the type of market you are in.
You must match your position to the opportunity.

2 Some campaigns can be blunted.
Some campaigns are too bland.
Some campaigns stumble.
Some campaigns self-destruct.
Some campaigns are chaotic.
Some campaigns must be abandoned.

You must recognize these six campaign weaknesses.
They make it hard to take advantage of opportunities.
Your decisions create these weaknesses.

SYSTEMS:

Campaigns are systems in which the components must be put together to make sure that sales get made.

¹⁰One general can command a force equal to the enemy.
Still his enemy outflanks him.
This means that his army can be outmaneuvered.

¹³Another can have strong soldiers but weak officers.
This means that his army is too lax.

¹⁵Another has strong officers but weak soldiers.
This means that his army will fall down.

¹⁷Another has subcommanders that are angry and defiant.
They attack the enemy and fight their own battles.
The commander cannot know the battlefield.
This means that his army will fall apart.

²¹Another general is weak and easygoing.
He fails to make his orders clear.
His officers and men lack direction.
This shows in his military formations.
This means that his army is disorganized.

²⁶Another general fails to predict the enemy.
He pits his small forces against larger ones.
His weak forces attack stronger ones.
He fails to pick his fights correctly.
This means that his army must retreat.

COMMAND:

Only one person makes the key decisions in an organization, thereby shaping it and creating any flaws.

Your market resources may be equal to the competition's.
However, a competitor leverages your weaknesses against you.
This means that your campaign can be blunted.

Your communication channels are good, but your message is weak.
This means that your campaign is too bland.

Your message is strong, but your communication is weak.
This means that your campaign will stumble.

Your marketing partners are excitable and undisciplined.
They want to sell to any market they can find.
Then your organization cannot focus on its target market.
This means that your campaign will self-destruct.

Some marketing is lazy and sloppy.
You fail to make your product's position unique.
Your marketing and communication lack focus.
This shows in the lack of a clear direction.
This means that your campaign is chaotic.

Some marketing fails to account for the competition.
You pit a weak message against a stronger one.
You pit limited channels against superior ones.
You fail to identify your best prospects.
This means that your campaign must be abandoned.

BALANCE:

A campaign must balance positioning, communication, message, focus, and competitive thinking.

³¹You must know all about these six weaknesses.
You must understand the philosophies that lead to defeat.
When a general arrives, you can know what he will do.
You must study each general carefully.

You must control your field position. 3
It will always strengthen your army.

³You must predict the enemy to overpower him and win.
You must analyze the obstacles, dangers, and distances.
This is the best way to command.

⁶Understand your field position before you go to battle.
Then you will win.
You can fail to understand your field position and still fight.
Then you will lose.

¹⁰You must provoke battle when you will certainly win.
It doesn't matter what you are ordered.
The government may order you not to fight.
Despite that, you must always fight when you will win.

FORESIGHT:

*Once you can
quickly diagnose
a situation, you
know the appro-
priate response
when others
leave openings.*

¹⁴Sometimes provoking a battle will lead to a loss.
The government may order you to fight.
Despite that, you must avoid battle when you will
lose.

You must understand all six of these campaign weaknesses.
You must understand the thinking behind them.
When you face competitors, you must recognize their weaknesses.
Your opportunities come from knowing their weaknesses.

3 You must shape your market position.
It must generate revenues for your company.

You must foresee how to outmaneuver competitors.
You must recognize the types of problems in an opportunity.
This is the only way to campaign.

Design your campaign to fit the nature of your opportunities.
This is how you make money.
You can campaign without understanding the opportunity.
This will always cost you money.

Challenge competitors when they are at a disadvantage.
Forget your original marketing plans.
You may not have planned on a certain opportunity.
You must go after markets when the opportunity is right.

Know when a market battle will be unprofitable.
Your company may desire that market.
Still, you must avoid campaigns that cost you more
than they gain.

FLEXIBILITY:

As you learn more about your market situation, you must be willing to adapt your plans accordingly.

¹⁷You must advance without desiring praise.
You must retreat without fearing shame.
The only correct move is to preserve your troops.
This is how you serve your country.
This is how you reward your nation.

Think of your soldiers as little children. 4
You can make them follow you into a deep river.
Treat them as your beloved children.
You can lead them all to their deaths.

⁵Some leaders are generous but cannot use their men.
They love their men but cannot command them.
Their men are unruly and disorganized.
These leaders create spoiled children.
Their soldiers are useless.

You may know what your soldiers will do in an attack. 5
You may not know if the enemy is vulnerable to attack.
You will then win only half the time.
You may know that the enemy is vulnerable to attack.
You may not know if your men have the capability of
attacking him.
You will still win only half the time.
You may know that the enemy is vulnerable to attack.
You may know that your men are ready to attack.
You may not, however, know how to position yourself in the
field for battle.
You will still win only half the time.

Campaigns must pay off, not just create name recognition.
Abandon without embarrassment campaigns that don't pay off.
The only goal is to increase your profits.
This is how you build your organization.
This is how you ensure your success.

4 Think of your marketing partners as your family.
They will support you in an uncertain future.
Develop partnerships with care and understanding.
They will serve you faithfully.

Some spend the money but do not care about their partners.
They like partnerships but do not take a leadership role in them.
This results in confused and unproductive relationships.
You cannot be unclear about partner responsibilities.
Such partnerships are useless.

5 You can know how to respond to a type of market opportunity.
You may not recognize when that opportunity arises.
If you do not, your marketing is incomplete.
You can recognize a market opportunity when it arises.
However, you must also know exactly how to take advantage of that
type of opportunity.
If you do not, your marketing is incomplete.
You can recognize a market opportunity when it arises.
You can know how to respond to that type of market opportunity.
However, you must also know exactly how to position your com-
pany against the competition.
If you do not, your marketing is incomplete.

[11]You must know how to make war.
You can then act without confusion.
You can attempt anything.

[14]We say:
Know the enemy and know yourself.
Your victory will be painless.
Know the weather and the field.
Your victory will be complete.

✦ ✦ ✦

RELATIVITY:

Strategically, all your qualities, both good and bad, arise only in comparison with your opponents.

You must know how to meet the competition.
Your path is then completely certain.
You cannot make mistakes.

Warrior marketing says:
Know your competitors and your capabilities.
Then profits are easy.
Understand market trends and your opportunities.
Then your profits are assured.

◆ ◆ ◆

SYNTHESIS:

*Warrior market-
ing acknowl-
edges that we
cannot know
everything but
that we must
master a few
key elements.*

Related Articles from *Sun Tzu's Playbook*

In chapter ten, Sun Tzu discusses the use of temporary positions in building relation-ships with voters. To learn the step-by-step techniques involved, we recommend the Sun Tzu's Art of War Playbook *articles listed below.*

2.3 Personal Interactions: making progress through personal interactions.

2.3.1 Action and Reaction: how we advance based on how others reaction to our actions.

2.3.2 Reaction Unpredictability: why we can never exactly predict the react of others.

2.3.3 Likely Reactions: the range of potential reactions in gathering information.

2.3.4 Using Questions: using questions in gathering information and predicting reactions.

4.5 Opportunity Surfaces: judging potential opportunities from a distance.

4.5.1 Surface Area: choosing opportunities on the basis of their size.

4.5.2 Surface Barriers: how to select opportunities by evaluating obstacles.

4.5.3 Surface Holding Power: sticky and slippery situations.

4.6 Six Benchmarks: simplifying the comparisons of opportunities.

4.6.1 Spread-Out Conditions: recognizing opportunities that are too large.

4.6.2 Constricted Conditions: identifying and using constricted positions.

4.6.3 Barricaded Conditions: the issues related to the extremes of obstacles.

4.6.4 Wide-Open Conditions: the issues related to an absence of barriers.

4.6.5 Fixed Conditions: positions with extreme holding power.

4.6.6 Sensitive Conditions: positions with no holding power on pursuing opportunities.

4.7 Competitive Weakness: how certain opportunities can bring out our weaknesses.

4.7.1 Command Weaknesses: the character flaws of leaders and how to exploit them.

4.7.2 Group Weaknesses: organizational weakness and where groups fail.

4.8 Climate Support: choosing new positions based on future changes.

4.9 Opportunity Mapping: two-dimensional tool for comparing opportunity probabilities.

Scattering.

Easy.

Disputed.

Open

Intersecting.

Dangerous.   Confined

Bad.

Deadly

Chapter 11

九地

Types of Terrain – Stages

The science of strategy predicts that marketing programs will evolve over time. Marketing campaigns tend to pass through nine different stages. While not every campaign goes through each of these stages, the strategic situations that they represent are extremely common.

Each of these stages in the development of a marketing campaign has its own clear tactical focus. As the marketing effort continues toward winning a profitable position in a target market, you have to adjust your tactics to match the stage of your campaign's development. This chapter's first section describes the nine campaign stages and the specific tactical responses that they require.

The longer a given campaign takes to win its market, the more difficult the challenges that it faces. The nine campaign stages fall into three general groups. Early stages demand focus and concentration. Middle stages demand good management and organization. Later stages demand creativity and perseverance.

Good marketing demands appropriate leadership at each stage of a campaign. The evolution of a campaign through these stages depends largely on human psychology. People respond in a predictable way as campaigns continue without clear resolution.

Knowledge and unity are the keys to successfully concluding a campaign. Over time, you must especially develop the ability to recover from setbacks. Because you never know how long a campaign can take, you need to set the proper tone at the very start.

The Art of War: Types of Terrain

SUN TZU SAID:

Use the art of war. 1
Know when the terrain will scatter you.
Know when the terrain will be easy.
Know when the terrain will be disputed.
Know when the terrain is open.
Know when the terrain is intersecting.
Know when the terrain is dangerous.
Know when the terrain is bad.
Know when the terrain is confined.
Know when the terrain is deadly.

GROUND:

Ground, territory, and terrain are all from the same Chinese concept, "di," which also means situation and condition.

11Warring parties must sometimes fight inside their
own territory.
This is scattering terrain.

13When you enter hostile territory, your penetration
is shallow.
This is easy terrain.

15Some terrain gives you an advantageous position.
But it gives others an advantageous position as well.
This will be disputed terrain.

The Art of Marketing: Stages

A MARKETING WARRIOR HEARS:

1 Use your warrior marketing:
Know when the campaign's stage is tenuous.
Know when the campaign's stage is easy.
Know when the campaign's stage is contentious.
Know when the campaign's stage is open.
Know when the campaign's stage is shared.
Know when the campaign's stage is serious.
Know when the campaign's stage is difficult.
Know when the campaign's stage is limiting.
Know when the campaign's stage is desperate.

You must sometimes defend against a new competitor
in your established market.
This is the tenuous stage of the campaign.

When you first explore a new market, initial success
comes quickly.
This is the easy stage of the campaign.

You discover market areas that offer tremendous opportunities.
However, many other people discover these opportunities as well.
This is the contentious stage of the campaign.

STAGES:

*The nine stages
described here
explain a logical
evolution that
campaigns go
through as they
continue.*

[18]You can use some terrain to advance easily.
Others can advance along with you.
This is open terrain.

[21]Everyone shares access to a given area.
The first one to arrive there can gather a larger group than
anyone else.
This is intersecting terrain.

[24]You can penetrate deeply into hostile territory.
Then many hostile cities are behind you.
This is dangerous terrain.

[27]There are mountain forests.
There are dangerous obstructions.
There are reservoirs.
Everyone confronts these obstacles on a campaign.
They make bad terrain.

[32]In some areas, the entry passage is narrow.
You are closed in as you try to get out of them.
In this type of area, a few people can effectively attack your
much larger force.
This is confined terrain.

[36]You can sometimes survive only if you fight quickly.
You will die if you delay.
This is deadly terrain.

The Art of Marketing: **Stages**

You make easy progress in the market.
Competitors are making easy progress in the market as well.
This is the open stage of the campaign.

Your products' sales depend on the sales of products from others.
The first group to put together an alliance to jointly market its products will succeed.
This is the shared stage of the campaign.

You have invested heavily in a campaign to win a market.
Opponents threaten to cut off your financial support.
This is the serious stage of the campaign.

A campaign runs into problems that slow it down.
It encounters serious barriers to winning a market.
Unforeseen changes take place.
The campaign encounters more problems as it continues.
This is the difficult stage of the campaign.

In some campaigns, you get into situations with few good options.
Your entire effort depends on a few key things going correctly.
Everything can be lost if your competitors discover how dependent you are.
This is the limiting stage of the campaign.

Sometimes you can win only if you commit all your resources.
The campaign will certainly fail if you delay.
This is the desperate stage of the campaign.

[39]To be successful, you must control scattering terrain by avoiding battle.

Control easy terrain by not stopping.

Control disputed terrain by not attacking.

Control open terrain by staying with the enemy's forces.

Control intersecting terrain by uniting with your allies.

Control dangerous terrain by plundering.

Control bad terrain by keeping on the move.

Control confined terrain by using surprise.

Control deadly terrain by fighting.

Go to an area that is known to be good for waging war. **2**
Use it to cut off the enemy's contact between his front and back lines.

Prevent his small parties from relying on his larger force.

Stop his strong divisions from rescuing his weak ones.

Prevent his officers from getting their men together.

Chase his soldiers apart to stop them from amassing.

Harass them to prevent their ranks from forming.

[8]When joining battle gives you an advantage, you must do it.

When it isn't to your benefit, you must avoid it.

CONTROL:

Each of the nine "terrains," "conditions," or "stages" demands a specific form of response.

[10]A daring soldier may ask:

"A large, organized enemy army and its general are coming.

What do I do to prepare for them?"

To be successful, adjust to the tenuous stage by not avoiding confrontations.
Adjust to the easy stage by keeping up the pressure.
Adjust to the contentious stage by avoiding confrontations.
Adjust to the open stage by keeping up with competitors.
Adjust to the shared stage by making quick alliances.
Adjust to the serious stage by focusing on generating income.
Adjust to the difficult stage by keeping the campaign going.
Adjust to the limiting stage by doing the unexpected.
Adjust to the desperate stage by meeting opponents directly.

2 Find the market areas where you are the most competitive.
Use niche marketing to prevent larger competitors from bringing their resources against you.
Choose niches where your competitors' size works against them.
Choose market areas where competitors have less knowledge.
Discourage competitors from focusing resources on your market.
Prevent successes that could bring them into your market.
Hamper their distribution and communication channels.

Challenging competitors to a comparison benefits you.
When it isn't in your benefit, avoid comparisons.

DIVISION:

Even courageous marketing warriors worry:
"Large, well-organized competitors are coming into my market.
What should I do?"

When marketing against specific competitors, you must try to split up their focus, resources, and positions.

¹³Tell him:
"First seize an area that the enemy must have.
Then he will pay attention to you.
Mastering speed is the essence of war.
Take advantage of a large enemy's inability to keep up.
Use a philosophy of avoiding difficult situations.
Attack the area where he doesn't expect you."

You must use the philosophy of an invader. 3
Invade deeply and then concentrate your forces.
This controls your men without oppressing them.

⁴Get your supplies from the riches of the territory.
It is sufficient to supply your whole army.

⁶Take care of your men and do not overtax them.
Your esprit de corps increases your momentum.
Keep your army moving and plan for surprises.
Make it difficult for the enemy to count your forces.
Position your men where there is no place to run.
They will then face death without fleeing.
They will find a way to survive.
Your officers and men will fight to their utmost.

¹⁴Military officers who are committed lose their fear.
When they have nowhere to run, they must stand firm.
Deep in enemy territory, they are captives.
Since they cannot escape, they will fight.

There is an answer.
You go after customers that these competitors need to maintain.
Then your larger competitors must worry about their own market.
You can change your targets more quickly than they can respond.
Threaten one area of their markets and move on to another.
You do not want to get into a marketing battle for these markets.
You harass unprotected parts of their markets to protect your own.

3 Your marketing must target moving into new markets.
Commit yourself to new markets and focus resources on them.
Your organization must be united in its effort to win these markets.

You must generate income quickly from a new market.
Only sales can pay for your marketing efforts.

Husband your marketing resources and do not overspend.
Create a market image that fuels your future success.
Keep your campaign going and expect problems.
Prevent competitors from knowing how much you can invest.
People in the campaign must depend financially on its success.
They will then solve problems instead of making excuses.
They will discover how to make it work.
You must get the most out of every decision and resource.

Get commitments to the campaign to tie people to you.
When people don't have excuses, they must make a stand.
The more deeply involved people are, the more dedicated they are.
People are effective when they aren't thinking about their options.

[18]Commit your men completely.
Without being posted, they will be on guard.
Without being asked, they will get what is needed.
Without being forced, they will be dedicated.
Without being given orders, they can be trusted.

[23]Stop them from guessing by removing all their doubts.
Stop them from dying by giving them no place to run.

[25]Your officers may not be rich.
Nevertheless, they still desire plunder.
They may die young.
Nevertheless, they still want to live forever.

[29]You must order the time of attack.
Officers and men may sit and weep until their lapels are wet.
When they stand up, tears may stream down their cheeks.
Put them in a position where they cannot run.
They will show the greatest courage under fire.

Make good use of war. 4
This demands instant reflexes.
You must develop these instant reflexes.
Act like an ordinary mountain snake.
If people strike your head then stop them with your tail.
If they strike your tail then stop them with your head.
If they strike your middle then use both your head and tail.

Totally commit your organization to the campaign's focus.
Without being warned, everyone must be on guard.
Without being asked, everyone must do what is needed.
Without being forced, everyone must be dedicated.
Without being told, everyone must concentrate.

Stop any second-guessing by making the commitment clear.
Avoid failure by leaving your people no excuses.

Your people and partners may not be rich.
This is not because they do not want to win wealth.
You may all fail.
It should not be because you did not commit to success.

You must establish a deadline for commitments.
Everyone will complain and cry that they cannot meet the deadlines.
When they have to act, they will tell you that they cannot.
Put them in a position where they have no choice.
They will find a way to get the work done.

4 Know what campaign stage you are in.
Marketing demands quick responses.
You must prepare to overcome campaign problems instantly.
You should be able to act on instinct.
If attacked at the campaign's beginning, you can win in the end.
If challenged at the end, you can win by having a good beginning.
If threatened in between, win by having a good beginning and end.

[8]A daring soldier asks:
"Can any army imitate these instant reflexes?"
We answer:
"It can."

[12]To command and get the most out of proud people, you
must study adversity.
People work together when they are in the same boat
during a storm.
In this situation, one rescues the other just as the
right hand helps the left.

[15]Use adversity correctly.
Tether your horses and bury your wagon's wheels.
Still, you can't depend on this alone.
An organized force is braver than lone individuals.
This is the art of organization.
Put the tough and weak together.
You must also use the terrain.

ADVERSITY:

*Strategically,
unity is strength,
and nothing
unites a force
more than being
threatened by a
common enemy.*

[22]Make good use of war.
Unite your men as one.
Never let them give up.

The commander must be a military professional. 5
This requires confidence and detachment.
You must maintain dignity and order.
You must control what your men see and hear.
They must follow you without knowing your plans.

You may question these responses.
Can warrior marketing foresee all possible situations?
There is only one answer.
It can.

Your ability to secure market leadership depends on creating a
common enemy.
You must join with your target market by accepting its
problems as your own.
You and your customers should work together as partners to solve the market's problems.

Share your customers' worries.
Tie your future together with theirs.
Even this is not enough.
Partners are more courageous than lone companies.
This is the art of collaborating.
You must help your weakest customers the most.
You must use your market leverage.

Make good use of campaigning.
Unite with your customers.
Never give up on them.

LEADERSHIP:

*You position
yourself for
leadership when
your decision-
making focuses
on your market-
place's concerns.*

5 You must run a campaign like a marketing leader.
This requires confidence and detachment.
You must maintain your leadership and focus.
You must control what your marketplace sees and hears.
Markets must trust you without knowing your condition.

⁶You can reinvent your men's roles.

You can change your plans.

You can use your men without their understanding.

⁹You must shift your campgrounds.

You must take detours from the ordinary routes.

You must use your men without giving them your strategy.

¹²A commander provides what is needed now.

This is like climbing high and being willing to kick away your ladder.

You must be able to lead your men deeply into different surrounding territory.

And yet, you can discover the opportunity to win.

¹⁶You must drive men like a flock of sheep.

You must drive them to march.

You must drive them to attack.

You must never let them know where you are headed.

You must unite them into a great army.

You must then drive them against all opposition.

This is the job of a true commander.

²³You must adapt to the different terrain.

You must adapt to find an advantage.

You must manage your people's affections.

You must study all these skills.

You must reinvent marketing messages.
You can redefine your product position.
You must lead because you have more knowledge.

You must change your market position.
You must look for different ways to advance that position.
You must use partnerships without becoming predictable.

Make your marketing decisions based on current opportunities.
You must be willing to go out on a limb to put yourself in a position to expand.
You must be trusted well enough to invest heavily in an untried but closely related market.
This is how you uncover big new markets.

You must make your marketing team work as a group.
You must force them to meet deadlines.
You must challenge them to be aggressive.
Don't make long-term plans for a campaign's direction.
You must focus the team on the task at hand.
You must push them to meet the competition.
This is the job of a true marketing manager.

You must respond to every campaign stage.
You must use the right approach to win the market.
You must win your marketing team's respect.
You must know all the appropriate responses.

Always use the philosophy of invasion. 6
Deep invasions concentrate your forces.
Shallow invasions scatter your forces.
When you leave your country and cross the border, you must
take control.
This is always critical ground.
You can sometimes move in any direction.
This is always intersecting ground.
You can penetrate deeply into a territory.
This is always dangerous ground.
You penetrate only a little way.
This is always easy ground.
Your retreat is closed and the path ahead tight.
This is always confined ground.
There is sometimes no place to run.
This is always deadly ground.

[16]To use scattering terrain correctly, you must inspire your
men's devotion.
On easy terrain, you must keep in close communication.
On disputed terrain, you must hamper the enemy's progress.
On open terrain, you must carefully defend your chosen position.
On intersecting terrain, you must solidify your alliances.
On dangerous terrain, you must ensure your food supplies.
On bad terrain, you must keep advancing along the road.
On confined terrain, you must stop information leaks from
your headquarters.
On deadly terrain, you must show what you can do by
killing the enemy.

6 Your campaign must generate income from its target market.
Total commitment to your target market focuses your efforts.
Halfhearted commitments dissipate your resources.
At the beginning of a campaign in a new market, you must take the lead.
This is a critical time.
Your interests sometimes join with those of other organizations.
You must create good partnerships.
You can invest everything in the campaign for a new market.
This is always the serious stage.
All markets look promising when you first start in them.
This is always the easy part of the campaign.
A campaign can narrow until options are limited.
This is the limiting stage of the campaign.
A campaign can run out of options.
This is the desperate stage.

To succeed in the tenuous stage, you must be a missionary for your organization's mission.
In the easy stage, you must focus on strong communications.
In the contentious stage, you must create obstacles for your competitors.
In the open stage, you must maintain your market leadership.
In the shared stage, you must join with the best partners.
In the serious stage, you must focus on generating income.
In the difficult stage, you must keep the campaign going.
In the limiting stage, you must keep your predicament and solution a secret.
In the desperate stage, you must prove yourself by winning your target market.

²⁵Make your men feel like an army.
Surround them and they will defend themselves.
If they cannot avoid it, they will fight.
If they are under pressure, they will obey.

Do the right thing when you don't know your 7
different enemies' plans.
Don't attempt to meet them.

³You don't know the position of mountain forests, dangerous
obstructions, and reservoirs?
Then you cannot march the army.
You don't have local guides?
You won't get any of the benefits of the terrain.

⁷There are many factors in war.
You may lack knowledge of any one of them.
If so, it is wrong to take a nation into war.

¹⁰You must be able to control your government's war.
If you divide a big nation, it will be unable to put together a
large force.
Increase your enemy's fear of your ability.
Prevent his forces from getting together and
organizing.

KNOWLEDGE:

*Strategy teaches
that you can
replace invest-
ment of time
and effort with
more complete
information.*

Make your marketing team successful.
Make them protect their market to protect their income.
When they have no choice, they will work.
When they are pressured, they will follow your lead.

7 Do the right thing when you do not understand your competitors' market direction.
Do not try to challenge them in the market.

You must know the industry issues, business problems, and trends in the marketplace.
Campaigns must avoid foreseeable obstacles.
Hire those who know the marketplace.
You need to know how leverage opportunities in the market.

Continually reevaluate the key factors of the marketplace.
Systematically reexamine each of them.
Otherwise, you cannot invest in a marketing campaign.

You must unite your organization in its market focus.
Meanwhile, think of ways to divide your competitors'
market focus.
Keep competitors worried about what you are doing.
Hamper their ability to focus on their own programs
and campaigns.

REEVALUATE:

Market analysis must be repeated constantly as you reexamine the five key factors that define your position.

14Do the right thing and do not arrange outside alliances
before their time.
You will not have to assert your authority prematurely.
Trust only yourself and your self-interest.
This increases the enemy's fear of you.
You can make one of his allies withdraw.
His whole nation can fall.

20Distribute rewards without worrying about having a system.
Halt without the government's command.
Attack with the whole strength of your army.
Use your army as if it were a single man.

24Attack with skill.
Do not discuss it.
Attack when you have an advantage.
Do not talk about the dangers.
When you can launch your army into deadly ground, even if
it stumbles, it can still survive.
You can be weakened in a deadly battle and yet be stronger
afterward.

30Even a large force can fall into misfortune.
If you fall behind, however, you can still turn defeat into victory.
You must use the skills of war.
To survive, you must adapt yourself to your enemy's purpose.
You must stay with him no matter where he goes.
It may take a thousand miles to kill the general.
If you correctly understand him, you can find the skill to do it.

Do not make the mistake of depending too heavily upon your marketing partnerships.
You do not want to have to fight for your decisions.
Trust yourself and your own resources.
This decreases your competitors' sources of information.
You may convince your competitors' allies to abandon them.
Their whole campaign may then collapse.

Reward people according to their accomplishments.
Stop what isn't working without getting approval from others.
Focus all your resources on your target market.
You cannot disperse your resources.

Move into new markets carefully.
Do not reveal your plans.
Leverage any advantage you find to penetrate your market.
Do not advertise the potential problems.
You can go through difficult stages and lose customers, but you can still survive.
You may lose ground in a competitive market, but you can also learn from your mistakes.

You can be in a great position and still get into bad situations.
If you make mistakes, you can turn initial failure into success.
This is the role of strategy.
Market survival depends on knowing your competitors' direction.
You must keep up with your competitors to compete with them.
You can make fast progress and overtake a market leader.
If you understand your competitors, you can find an opportunity.

Manage your government correctly at the start of a war. **8**
Close your borders and tear up passports.
Block the passage of envoys.
Encourage politicians at headquarters to stay out of it.
You must use any means to put an end to politics.
Your enemy's people will leave you an opening.
You must instantly invade through it.

[8]Immediately seize a place that they love.
Do it quickly.
Trample any border to pursue the enemy.
Use your judgment about when to fight.

[12]Doing the right thing at the start of war is like approaching a woman.
Your enemy's men must open the door.
After that, you should act like a streaking rabbit.
The enemy will be unable to catch you.

BEGINNINGS:

The start of a campaign is a delicate time when you set the direction for the entire course of the campaign.

8 Prepare your organization at the start of a campaign.
Defend existing markets and keep competitors out.
Avoid negotiations with your competitors.
Keep nonmarketing people out of marketing decisions.
Eliminate anything that disturbs your organization's focus.
Identify your competitors' weaknesses.
Quickly take advantage of those weaknesses.

Quickly win a customer base in your target market.
Waste no time.
Redefine the market to the group of customers you can win.
Use your best judgment about where to compete.

Success at the beginning comes from wooing your target customers
like a man would woo a woman.
Your competitors will eventually neglect their customers.
When they do, you must act quickly.
Never let your competitors catch up with you.

♦ ♦ ♦

OPENINGS:

*You cannot win
markets without
the cooperation
of competitors
who leave you
the opening that
you need.*

Related Articles from *Sun Tzu's Playbook*

In chapter eleven, Sun Tzu explains instant situation response. To learn the step-by-step techniques involved, we recommend the Sun Tzu's Art of War Playbook *articles listed below.*

6.0 Situation Response: selecting the actions most appropriate to a situation.

6.1 Situation Recognition: situation recognition in making advances.

6.1.1 Conditioned Reflexes: how we develop automatic, instantaneous responses.

6.1.2 Prioritizing Conditions: parsing complex competitive conditions into simple responses.

6.2 Campaign Evaluation: how we justify continued investment in an ongoing campaign.

6.2.1 Campaign Flow: seeing campaigns as a series of situations that flow logically from one to another.

6.2.2 Campaign Goals: assessing the value of a campaign by a larger mission.

6.3 Campaign Patterns: how knowing campaign stages gives us insight into our situation.

6.3.1 Early-Stage Situations: the common situations that arise the earliest in campaigns.

6.3.2 Middle-Stage Situations: how progress creates transitional situations in campaigns.

6.3.3 Late-Stage Situations: understanding the final and most dangerous stages of campaigns.

6.4 Nine Situations: the nine common competitive situations.

6.4.1 Dissipating Situations: situations where defensive unity is destroyed.

6.4.2 Easy Situations: recognizing situations of easy initial progress.

6.4.3 Contentious Situations: identifying situations that invite conflict.

6.4.4 Open Situations: recognizing situations that are races without a course.

6.4.5 Intersecting Situations: recognizing situations that bring people together.

6.4.6 Serious Situations: identifying situations where resources can be cut off.

6.4.7 Difficult Situations: recognizing situations where serious barriers must be overcome.

6.4.8 Limited Situations: identifying situations defined by a bottleneck.

6.4.9 Desperate Situations: identifying situations where destruction is possible.

6.5 Nine Responses: using the best responses to the nine common competitive situations.

6.5.1 Dissipating Response: responding to dissipation by the use of offense as defense.

6.5.2 Easy Response: responding to easy situations by overcoming complacency.

6.5.3 Contentious Response: responding to contentious situations by knowing how to avoid conflict.

6.5.4 Open Response: responding to open situations by keeping up with the opposition.

6.5.5 Intersecting Response: the formation of situational alliances.

6.5.6 Serious Response: responding to serious situations by finding immediate income.

6.5.7 Difficult Response: the role of persistence in responding to difficult situations.

6.5.8 Limited Response: the need for secret speed in limited situations.

6.5.9 Desperate Response: using all our resources in responding to desperate situations.

6.6 Campaign Pause: knowing when to stop advancing a position.

Chapter 12

火攻

Attacking With Fire – Desires

Classical strategy demands that you leverage conditions in the environment against your opponents. In adapting this philosophy, warrior marketing starts with the idea that you cannot create the environmental situations that you need. The competitive environment is bigger and more powerful than your ability to control it. Instead, you must study the environment and use the conditions that you find. This lesson is critical in understanding and using market desires to accomplish your goals.

Sun Tzu uses this chapter to discuss a specific environmental force—fire—because he considers it the most dangerous and unpredictable force in the physical environment. In the context of marketing, this chapter serves as a guide to leveraging customer desires, which are the most dangerous and unpredictable force in marketing. The insatiable and ever-shifting desires of customers can reshape the environment quickly, given the right conditions.

The chapter begins by discussing the five specific types of desires that we can leverage in a marketplace. Conditions and the timing must be exactly right to open these targets to our advantage. Even then, the attack itself is less important than the responses to it. A change does not necessarily create an opening. It is people's responses to change that create opportunities.

The destructive force of fire and desire and our responses to them are the critical elements in safely using our market environment to dominate our competitors.

The Art of War: Attacking With Fire

SUN TZU SAID:

There are five ways of attacking with fire. 1
The first is burning troops.
The second is burning supplies.
The third is burning supply transport.
The fourth is burning storehouses.
The fifth is burning camps.

7To make fire, you must have the resources.
To build a fire, you must prepare the raw materi-
als.

9To attack with fire, you must be in the right season.
To start a fire, you must have the time.

11Choose the right season.
The weather must be dry.

13Choose the right time.
Pick a season when the grass is as high as the side of a cart.

15You can tell the proper days by the stars in the night sky.
You want days when the wind rises in the morning.

The Art of Marketing: Desires

A MARKETING WARRIOR HEARS:

1 There are five categories of market desires.
The first is the need for safety.
The second is the need for comfort.
The third is the need for advancement.
The fourth is the need for wealth.
The fifth is the need for affection.

You need the products to address a certain desire.
To stimulate desire, you must know the market's needs.

To target a desire, your timing must be right.
To address a desire, you must take your time.

Learn the patterns in your marketplace.
Campaign when the customers are hungry.

Be careful of your timing.
Pick a time when your customer will be buying.

To know the right time, analyze your market research data.
Pick a time when pressure is building.

DESIRES:

The targets for using desire as a weapon are the same as the different types of resources people value.

Everyone attacks with fire. 2
You must create five different situations with fire and be able
to adjust to them.

3You start a fire inside the enemy's camp.
Then attack the enemy's periphery.

5You launch a fire attack, but the enemy remains calm.
Wait and do not attack.

7The fire reaches its height.
Follow its path if you can.
If you can't follow it, stay where you are.

REACTION:

The environment is unpredictable so you must always act based upon how situations develop rather than your plans.

10Spreading fires on the outside of camp can kill.
You can't always get fire inside the enemy's camp.
Take your time in spreading it.

13Set the fire when the wind is at your back.
Don't attack into the wind.
Daytime winds last a long time.
Night winds fade quickly.

17Every army must know how to adjust to the five
possible attacks by fire.
Use many men to guard against them.

2 Everyone tries to address market desires.
You must respond to the five types of desire and adjust your marketing approach.

You can spark a desire at the heart of a market.
Then you come into that market easily.

You target a need, but customers do not react quickly.
Wait for desire to build before investing in a campaign.

Some market desires peak quickly.
You must follow up on the interest.
If you cannot move quickly, do not move at all.

Articulating hidden desires can win markets.
Do this when you cannot address a core desire.
Take your time generating the feeling of need.

Let the competitive situation fan market desires.
Do not fight against prevailing attitudes.
Well-known needs are the most lasting.
Less visible needs can fade quickly.

You must master the previous five approaches to using market desires.
You defend your customers by guarding them.

CONTROL:

The less control you have over the way that others react, the more comtrol you must have over the way that you react .

When you use fire to assist your attacks, you are clever. 3
Water can add force to an attack.
You can also use water to disrupt an enemy.
It does not, however, take his resources.

You win in battle by getting the opportunity to attack. 4
It is dangerous if you fail to study how to accomplish this
achievement.
As commander, you cannot waste your opportunities.

[4]We say:
A wise leader plans success.
A good general studies it.
If there is little to be gained, don't act.
If there is little to win, do not use your men.
If there is no danger, don't fight.

[10]As leader, you cannot let your anger interfere with the success of your forces.
As commander, you cannot let yourself become
enraged before you go to battle.
Join the battle only when it is in your advantage
to act.
If there is no advantage in joining a battle, stay
put.

DECISION:

*Your decisions
must use the
emotion of
others. Your
emotions cannot
determine your
decisions.*

3 Leveraging market desires to generate sales is smart marketing.
Using any change can add force to your campaign.
You can use market change to put competitors at a disadvantage.
Change alone, however, does not take away competitors' sales.

4 You win in market competition by targeting unfulfilled needs.
You create competitors if you do not pay attention to satisfying
those needs.
Your decisions can create a competitor's opportunities.

Strategy teaches:
You use your knowledge to choose your course.
You must not forget what success really means.
If a market cannot make you money, do not target it.
If it cannot be profitable, do not waste your resources.
If the target customers lack real desire, do not sell to them.

You must never let your emotions affect the success of a marketing
campaign.
You must never go after a market simply because you
want to humble the competition.
Go up against the competition only when it is profitable to do so.
If you cannot make money in competition, stay out of
it.

SUCCESS:

*A great market-
ing campaign
is not one that
wins recogni-
tion. It is one
that makes a
great profit.*

[14]Anger can change back into happiness.

Rage can change back into joy.

A nation once destroyed cannot be brought back to life.

Dead men do not return to the living.

[18]This fact must make a wise leader cautious.

A good general is on guard.

[20]Your philosophy must be to keep the nation peaceful and the army intact.

EMOTION:

Emotional gratification is never the goal of a competition. You must never lose sight of your goals in the heat of battle.

Emotions change with time.
A frustrating campaign can still bring you success.
Resources do not come back to you once they have been wasted.
When money is wasted, it is lost forever.

Knowing this, you must be careful.
You must guard against your own desires.

Your desire must be to keep your company profitable and your markets intact.

✦ ✦ ✦

THE PAYOFF:

Desire, like all weapons, cuts both ways. Customer desires can be profit-able. Your own desires can be costly.

Related Articles from *Sun Tzu's Playbook*

In chapter twelve, Sun Tzu discusses the use of environmental weapons. To learn the step-by-step techniques involved, we recommend the Sun Tzu's Art of War Playbook *articles listed below.*

9.0 Understanding Vulnerability: the use of common environmental attacks.

9.1 Climate Vulnerability: our vulnerability to environmental crises arising from change.

9.1.1 Climate Rivals: how changing conditions create opponents.

9.1.2 Threat Development: how changing conditions create environmental threats.

9.2 Points of Vulnerability: our points of vulnerability during an environmental crisis.

9.2.1 Personnel Risk: the vulnerability of key individuals.

9.2.2 Immediate Resource Risk: the vulnerability of the resources required for immediate use.

9.2.3 Transportation/Communication Risk: how firestorms choke normal channels of movement and communication.

9.2.4 Asset Risk: the threats to our fixed assets.

9.2.5 Organizational Risk: targeting the roles and responsibilities within an organization.

9.3 Crisis Leadership: maintaining the support of our supporters during attacks.

9.3.1 Mutual Danger: how we use mutual danger to create mutual strength.

9.3.2 Message Control: communication methods to use during a crisis.

9.4 Crisis Defense: how vulnerabilities are exploited and defended during a crisis.

9.4.1 Division Defense: preventing organizational division during a crisis.

9.4.2 Panic Defense: preventing the mistakes arising from panic during a crisis.

9.4.3 Defending Openings: how to defend openings created by a crisis.

9.4.4 Defending Alliances: dealing with guilt by association.

9.4.5 Defensive Balance: using short-term conditions to tip the balance in a crisis.

9.5 Crisis Exploitation: how to successfully use an opponent's crisis.

9.5.1 Adversarial Opportunities: how our opponents' crises can create opportunities.

9.5.2 Avoiding Emotion: the danger of exploiting environmental vulnerabilities for purely emotion reasons.

9.6 Constant Vigilance: where to focus our attention to preserve our positions.

Knowing

Chapter 13

用 間

Using Spies — Intelligence

This final chapter addresses the most important and delicate element of strategy: developing good sources for sensitive information. For marketing professionals, the lessons here about acquiring and utilizing market intelligence are invaluable. While you can gather valuable market research from generally available public sources, the market intelligence addressed in this chapter specifically means acquiring information that is not available to everyone.

The value of information can only be understood in the large context of the costs of market competition. The many different costs of marketing can be dramatically minimized by knowing how to gather the right information.

The critical marketing information that you need can only come from developing a network of people in the marketplace who act as your intelligence sources. There are five different types of market intelligence that you need. Each type of information requires a different type of intelligence source.

After developing a marketing intelligence network, you must know how to evaluate the information you receive and manage the needs of your information sources. Before you undertake a specific marketing campaign, you must first find sources that provide a complete picture of the challenges you will likely face.

The history of competition shows that victory goes to those who are the most successful at being the first to cultivate the best sources of market intelligence.

The Art of War: **Using Spies**

SUN TZU SAID:

All successful armies require thousands of men. 1
They invade and march thousands of miles.
Whole families are destroyed.
Other families must be heavily taxed.
Every day, a large amount of money must be spent.

⁶Internal and external events force people to move.
They are unable to work while on the road.
They are unable to find and hold a useful job.
This affects 70 percent of thousands of families.

¹⁰You can watch and guard for years.
Then a single battle can determine victory in a day.
Despite this, bureaucrats worship the value of
their salary money too dearly.
They remain ignorant of the enemy's condition.
The result is cruel.

¹⁵They are not leaders of men.
They are not servants of the state.
They are not masters of victory.

ECONOMICS:

The science of strategy is based on the idea that better information can be used to eliminate other costs.

The Art of Marketing: **Intelligence**

A MARKETING WARRIOR HEARS:

1 Building a market position requires resources.
You contact thousands of potential customers.
Most of that contact is wasted.
The company must pay for your efforts.
Every day, marketing consumes money.

Internal and external events force you to shift market position.
Every shift in position wastes more time and energy.
People do not necessarily know what is productive.
This confusion can eat away at your resources.

You can develop and defend your market for years.
You can lose it in a single day.
Despite this, many marketing people spend their
funds on luxuries instead of intelligence.
Many are surprised by a competitor's moves.
The result is devastating.

Without information, you cannot win a market.
You cannot support your company.
You cannot be successful.

INTELLIGENCE:

*Markets are
always domi-
nated by the
competitors that
have the best in-
formation about
customers.*

[18]You need a creative leader and a worthy commander.
You must move your troops to the right places to beat others.
You must accomplish your attack and escape unharmed.
This requires foreknowledge.
You can obtain foreknowledge.
You can't get it from demons or spirits.
You can't see it from professional experience.
You can't check it with analysis.
You can only get it from other people.
You must always know the enemy's situation.

You must use five types of spies. 2
You need local spies.
You need inside spies.
You need double agents.
You need doomed spies.
You need surviving spies.

[7]You need all five types of spies.
No one must discover your methods.
You will then be able to put together a true picture.
This is the commander's most valuable resource.

NETWORKS:

The key to gathering useful information is to have a range of different types of sources in your network.

[11]You need local spies.
Get them by hiring people from the countryside.

[13]You need inside spies.
Win them by subverting government officials.

You must be worthy to lead your marketplace.
You must use your resources wisely to win customers.
You must attack new segments without risking loss.
This requires information.
You can get this information.
You will not get it by luck or accident.
You will not get it from past experience.
You cannot reason out this information.
You can only get it by asking people questions.
You must always know what your customer is thinking.

2 You use five types of market intelligence.
You need information on target markets.
You need information on competitors' plans.
You need information on communication channels.
You need information on competitors' missteps.
You need information on market changes.

You must use all five types of intelligence.
If you do, no one will ever challenge your knowledge.
You can learn about any market and its workings.
This information is your most valuable resource.

You need information on your target market.
Get information by hiring experts from the market.

You need information on competitors' plans.
Find competitors' employees and hire them away.

INDIVIDUALS:

You need to build personal relationships to get the intelligence that makes a competitive difference.

¹⁵You need double agents.
Discover enemy agents and convert them.

¹⁷You need doomed spies.
Deceive professionals into being captured.
Let them know your orders.
They then take those orders to your enemy.

²¹You need surviving spies.
Someone must return with a report.

Your job is to build a complete army. 3
No relations are as intimate as the ones with spies.
No rewards are too generous for spies.
No work is as secret as that of spies.

⁵If you aren't clever and wise, you can't use spies.
If you aren't fair and just, you can't use spies.
If you can't see the small subtleties, you won't get the truth
from spies.

⁸Pay attention to small, trifling details!
Spies are helpful in every area.

¹⁰Spies are the first to hear information, so they must not
spread information.
Spies who give your location or talk to others must be killed
along with those to whom they have talked.

The Art of Marketing: Intelligence

You need information on communication channels.
Find the competition's resources and win them over.

You need information on your competitors' mistakes.
Mislead competitors into revealing them to you.
Trade your insights with them.
Make sure the insights you give them are misleading.

You need information on market changes.
Get it from good sales reporting.

3 Your job is to develop a complete marketing campaign.
No resources are as critical as your intelligence sources.
No reward is too generous for good information.
No information is as confidential as your research findings.

You must be perceptive to see the patterns in information.
You must be open and unbiased to evaluate intelligence.
If you are not sensitive to subtleties, you will not find the truth in
what people tell you.

You must pay close attention to small details.
Inside information is helpful in every decision.

Your market intelligence generates organizational knowledge but
your people must not spread information.
People who divulge your plans or position to the competition can
destroy you.

You may want to attack an army's position. 4
You may want to attack a certain fortification.
You may want to kill people in a certain place.
You must first know the guarding general.
You must know his left and right flanks.
You must know his hierarchy.
You must know the way in.
You must know where different people are stationed.
You must demand this information from your spies.

[10]You want to know the enemy spies in order to convert them into your men.
You find a source of information and bribe them.
You must bring them in with you.
You must obtain them as double agents and use them as your emissaries.

[14]Do this correctly and carefully.
You can contact both local and inside spies and obtain their support.
Do this correctly and carefully.
You create doomed spies by deceiving professionals.
You can use them to give false information.
Do this correctly and carefully.
You must have surviving spies capable of bringing you information at the right time.

SPECIFICS:

The more specific your targets become, the more specific the information needed to win them.

4 You may want to undermine a competitor's image.
You may want to go after a specific customer.
You may want to win a certain distributor.
You must first know how decision-makers think.
You must know the structures of their organizations.
You must know corporate hierarchies.
You must know what unmet needs you can exploit.
You must know who the key players are.
You must get this information from your intelligence network.

You want to know who provides information for your competitors
and win them away.
You must be willing to pay for information.
You must win information sources over to your side.
You must convince valuable existing channels to become your
resources.

You must do this carefully.
You can get information from your target market and from competi-
tors and find out what they know.
You must also do this selectively.
You can obtain information about where competitors'
weaknesses are.
You can provide competitors with misinformation.
You must do this quietly.
You need detailed information on specific customers
at the appropriate time.

INSIDERS:

*Your goal is to
get inside the
information loop
used by your
customers or
competitors.*

[21]These are the five different types of intelligence work.
You must be certain to master them all.
You must be certain to create double agents.
You cannot afford to be too cost conscious in creating these
double agents.

This technique created the success of ancient Shang. 5
This is how the Shang held its dynasty.

[3]You must always be careful of your success.
Learn from Lu Ya of Shang.

[5]Be a smart commander and a good general.
You do this by using your best and brightest people for spying.
This is how you achieve the greatest success.
This is how you meet the necessities of war.
The whole army's position and ability to move depends on
these spies.

SOURCES:

*Strategy is the
science of lever-
aging informa-
tion sources.*

There are five different types of intelligence.
You must be certain to master them all.
You must be certain to understand distribution.
Any time that you spend gathering inside information is time well spent.

5 Information is the hidden basis for all success in marketing.
This is how companies have built marketing superiority.

You must always be cautious in your market investment.
Learn from your past successes.

You must be an informed and capable marketing warrior.
Your information sources must be the best and the brightest.
This is how you achieve the greatest market success.
This is how you satisfy the needs of your marketplace.
Your product position and ability to move into new markets depend on intelligence.

♦ ♦ ♦

SUCCESS:

Success is based only on access to superior knowl-edge.

Related Articles from *Sun Tzu's Playbook*

In his final chapter, Sun Tzu explains how to use information channels. To learn the step-by-step techniques involved, we recommend the Sun Tzu's Art of War Playbook articles listed below.

2.0.0 Developing Perspective: adding depth to competitive analysis.

2.1 Information Value: knowledge and communication as the basis of strategy.

2.1.1 Information Limits: making good decisions with limited information.

2.1.3 Strategic Deception: misinformation and disinformation in competition.

2.1.4 Surprise: how the creation of surprise depends on the nature of information.

2.2 Information Gathering: gathering competitive information.

2.2.1 Personal Relationships: why information depends on personal relationships.

2.2.3 Standard Terminology: how mental models must be shared to enable communication.

2.3 Personal Interactions: making progress through personal interactions.

2.3.4 Using Questions: using questions in gathering information and predicting reactions.

2.3.5 Infinite Loops: predicting reactions on the basis of the "you-know-that-I-know-that-you-know" problem.

2.3.6 Promises and Threats: the use of promises and threats as strategic moves.

2.4 Contact Networks: the range of contacts needed to create perspective.

2.4.1 Ground Perspective: getting information on a new competitive arena.

2.4.2 Climate Perspective: getting perspective on temporary external conditions.

2.4.3 Command Perspective: developing sources for understanding decision-makers.

2.4.4 Methods Perspective: developing contacts who understand best practices.

2.4.5 Mission Perspective: how we develop and use a perspective on motivation.

2.5 The Big Picture: building big-picture strategic awareness.

2.6 Knowledge Leverage: getting competitive value out of knowledge.

2.7 Information Secrecy: defining the role of secrecy in relationships.

Glossary of Key Strategic Concepts

This glossary is keyed to the most common English words used in the translation of *The Art of War*. Those terms only capture the strategic concepts generally. Though translated as English nouns, verbs, adverbs, or adjectives, the Chinese characters on which they are based are totally conceptual, not parts of speech. For example, the character for CONFLICT is translated as the noun "conflict," as the verb "fight," and as the adjective "disputed." Ancient written Chinese was a conceptual language, not a spoken one. More like mathematical terms, these concepts are primarily defined by the strict structure of their relationships with other concepts. The Chinese names shown in parentheses with the characters are primarily based on Pinyin, but we occasionally use Cantonese terms to make each term unique.

ADVANCE (JEUN 進): to move into new GROUND; to expand your POSITION; to move forward in a campaign; the opposite of FLEE.

ADVANTAGE, *benefit* (LI 利): an opportunity arising from having a better POSITION relative to an ENEMY; an opening left by an ENEMY; a STRENGTH that matches against an ENEMY'S WEAKNESS; where fullness meets emptiness; a desirable characteristic of a strategic POSITION.

AIM, *vision, foresee* (JIAN 見): FOCUS on a specific ADVANTAGE, opening, or opportunity; predicting movements of an ENEMY; a skill of a LEADER in observing CLIMATE.

ANALYSIS, *plan* (GAI 計): a comparison of relative POSITION; the examination of the five factors that define a strategic POSITION; a combination of KNOWLEDGE and VISION; the ability to see through DECEPTION.

ARMY: see WAR.

ATTACK, *invade* (GONG 攻): a movement to new GROUND; advancing a strategic POSITION; action against an ENEMY in the sense of moving into his GROUND; opposite of DEFEND; does not necessarily mean CONFLICT.

BAD, *ruined* (PI 圮): a condition of the GROUND that makes ADVANCE difficult; destroyed; terrain that is broken and difficult to traverse; one of the nine situations or types of terrain.

BARRICADED: see OBSTACLES.

BATTLE (ZHAN 戰): to challenge; to engage an ENEMY; generically, to meet a challenge; to choose a confrontation with an ENEMY at a specific time and place; to focus all your resources on a task; to establish superiority in a POSITION; to challenge an ENEMY to increase CHAOS; that which is CONTROLLED by SURPRISE; one of the four forms of ATTACK; the response to a DESPERATE SITUATION; character meaning was originally "big meeting," though later took on the meaning "big weapon"; not necessarily CONFLICT.

BRAVERY, *courage* (YONG 勇): the ability to face difficult choices; the character quality that deals with the changes of CLIMATE; courage of conviction; willingness to act on vision; one of the six characteristics of a leader.

BREAK, *broken, divided* (PO 破): to DIVIDE what is COMPLETE; the absence of a UNITING PHILOSOPHY; the opposite of UNITY.

CALCULATE, *count* (SHU 數): mathematical comparison of quantities and qualities; a measurement of DISTANCE or troop size.

CHANGE, *transform* (BIAN 變): transition from one CONDITION to another; the ability to adapt to different situations; a natural characteristic of CLIMATE.

CHAOS, *disorder* (JUAN 亂): CONDITIONS that cannot be FORESEEN; the natural state of confusion arising from BATTLE; one of six weaknesses of an organization; the opposite of CONTROL.

CLAIM, *position, form* (XING 形): to use the GROUND; a shape or specific condition of GROUND; the GROUND that you CONTROL; to use the benefits of the GROUND; the formations of troops; one of the four key skills in making progress.

CLIMATE, *heaven* (TIAN 天): the passage of time; the realm of uncontrollable CHANGE; divine providence; the weather; trends that CHANGE over time; generally, the future; what one must AIM at in the future; one of five key factors in ANALYSIS; the opposite of GROUND.

COMMAND (LING 令): to order or the act of ordering subordinates; the decisions of a LEADER; the creation of METHODS.

COMPETITION: see WAR.

COMPLETE: see UNITY.

CONDITION: see GROUND.

CONFINED, *surround* (WEI 圍): to encircle; a SITUATION or STAGE in which your options are limited; the proper tactic for dealing with an ENEMY that is ten times smaller; to seal off a smaller ENEMY; the characteristic of a STAGE in which a larger FORCE can be attacked by a smaller one; one of nine SITUATIONS or STAGES.

CONFLICT, *fight* (ZHENG 爭): to contend; to dispute; direct confrontation of arms with an ENEMY; highly desirable GROUND that creates disputes; one of nine types of GROUND, terrain, or stages.

CONSTRICTED, *narrow* (AI 狹): a confined space or niche; one of six field positions; the limited extreme of the dimension distance; the opposite of SPREAD-OUT.

CONTROL, *govern* (CHI 治): to manage situations; to overcome disorder; the opposite of CHAOS.

DANGEROUS: see SERIOUS.

DANGERS, *adverse* (AK 阨): a condition that makes it difficult to ADVANCE; one of three dimensions used to evaluate advantages; the dimension with the extreme field POSITIONS of ENTANGLING and SUPPORTING.

DEATH, *desperate* (SI 死): to end or the end of life or efforts; an extreme situation in which the only option is BATTLE; one of nine STAGES or types of TERRAIN; one of five types of SPIES; opposite of SURVIVE.

DECEPTION, *bluffing, illusion* (GUI 詭): to control perceptions; to control information; to mislead an ENEMY; an attack on an opponent's AIM; the characteristic of war that confuses perceptions.

DEFEND (SHOU 守): to guard or to hold a GROUND; to remain in a POSITION; the opposite of ATTACK.

DETOUR (YU 迂): the indirect or unsuspected path to a POSITION; the more difficult path to ADVANTAGE; the route that is not DIRECT.

DIRECT, *straight* (JIK 直): a straight or obvious path to a goal; opposite of DETOUR.

DISTANCE, *distant* (YUAN 遠): the space separating GROUND; to be remote from the current location; to occupy POSITIONS that are not close to one another; one of six field positions; one of the three dimensions for evaluating opportunities; the emptiness of space.

DIVIDE, *separate* (FEN 分): to break apart a larger force; to separate from a larger group; the opposite of JOIN and FOCUS.

DOUBLE AGENT, *reverse* (FAN 反): to turn around in direction; to change a situation; to switch a person's allegiance; one of five types of spies.

EASY, *light* (QING 輕): to require little effort; a SITUATION that requires little effort; one of nine STAGES or types of terrain; opposite of SERIOUS.

EMOTION, *feeling* (XIN 心): an unthinking reaction to AIM, a necessary element to inspire MOVES; a component of esprit de corps; never a sufficient cause for ATTACK.

ENEMY, *competitor* (DIK 敵): one who makes the same CLAIM; one with a similar GOAL; one with whom comparisons of capabilities are made.

ENTANGLING, *hanging* (GUA 懸): a POSITION that cannot be returned to; any CONDITION that leaves no easy place to go; one of six field positions.

EVADE, *avoid* (BI 避): the tactic used by small competitors when facing large opponents.

FALL APART, *collapse* (BENG 崩): to fail to execute good decisions; to fail to use a CONSTRICTED POSITION; one of six weaknesses of an organization.

FALL DOWN, *sink* (HAAM 陷): to fail to make good decisions; to MOVE from a SUPPORTING POSITION; one of six weaknesses of organizations.

FEELINGS, *affection, love* (CHING 情): the bonds of relationship; the result of a shared PHILOSOPHY; requires management.

FIGHT, *struggle* (DOU 鬥): to engage in CONFLICT; to face difficulties.

FIRE (HUO 火): an environmental weapon; a universal analogy for all weapons.

FLEE, *retreat, northward* (BEI 北): to abandon a POSITION; to surrender GROUND; one of six weaknesses of an ARMY; opposite of ADVANCE.

FOCUS, *concentrate* (ZHUAN 專): to bring resources together at a given time; to UNITE forces for a purpose; an attribute of having a shared PHILOSOPHY; the opposite of *divide*.

FORCE (LEI 力): power in the simplest sense; a GROUP of people bound by UNITY and FOCUS; the relative balance of STRENGTH in opposition to WEAKNESS.

FORESEE: see AIM.

FULLNESS: see STRENGTH.

GENERAL: see LEADER.

GOAL: see PHILOSOPHY.

GROUND, *situation, stage* (DI 地): the earth; a specific place; a specific condition; the place one competes; the prize of competition; one of five key factors in competitive analysis; the opposite of CLIMATE.

GROUPS, *troops* (DUI 隊): a number of people united under a shared PHILOSOPHY; human resources of an organization; one of the five targets of fire attacks.

INSIDE, *internal* (NEI 內): within a TERRITORY or organization; an insider; one of five types of spies; opposite of OUTSIDE.

INTERSECTING, *highway* (QU 衢): a SITUATION or GROUND that allows you to JOIN; one of nine types of terrain.

JOIN (HAP 合): to unite; to make allies; to create a larger FORCE; opposite of DIVIDE.

KNOWLEDGE, *listening* (ZHI 知): to have information; the result of listening; the first step in advancing a POSITION; the basis of strategy.

LAX, *loosen* (SHII 弛): too easygoing; lacking discipline; one of six weaknesses of an army.

LEADER, *general, commander* (JIANG 將): the decision-maker in a competitive unit; one who LISTENS and AIMS; one who manages TROOPS; superior of officers and men; one of the five key factors in analysis; the conceptual opposite of SYSTEM, the established methods, which do not require decisions.

LEARN, *compare* (XIAO 效): to evaluate the relative qualities of ENEMIES.

LISTEN, *obey* (TING 聽): to gather KNOWLEDGE; part of ANALYSIS.

LISTENING: see KNOWLEDGE.

LOCAL, *countryside* (XIANG 鄉): the nearby GROUND; to have KNOWLEDGE of a specific GROUND; one of five types of SPIES.

MARSH (ZE 澤): GROUND where footing is unstable; one of the four types of GROUND; analogy for uncertain situations.

METHOD: see SYSTEM.

MISSION: see PHILOSOPHY.

MOMENTUM, *influence* (SHI 勢): the FORCE created by SURPRISE set up by STANDARDS; used with TIMING.

MOUNTAINS, *hill, peak* (SHAN 山): uneven GROUND; one of four types of GROUND; an analogy for all unequal SITUATIONS.

MOVE, *march, act* (HANG 行): action toward a position or goal.

NATION (GUO 國): the state; the productive part of an organization; the seat of political power; the entity that controls an ARMY or competitive part of the organization.

OBSTACLES, *barricaded* (XIAN 險): to have barriers; one of the three characteristics of the GROUND; one of six field positions; as a field position, opposite of UNOBSTRUCTED.

OPEN, *meeting, crossing* (JIAO 交): to share the same GROUND without conflict; to come together; a SITUATION that encourages a race; one of nine TERRAINS or STAGES.

OPPORTUNITY: see ADVANTAGE.

OUTMANEUVER (SOU 走): to go astray; to be FORCED into a WEAK POSITION; one of six weaknesses of an army.

OUTSIDE, *external* (WAI 外): not within a TERRITORY or ARMY; one who has a different perspective; one who offers an objective view; opposite of INTERNAL.

PHILOSOPHY, *mission, goals* (TAO 道): the shared GOALS that UNITE an ARMY; a system of thought; a shared viewpoint; literally "the way"; a way to work together; one of the five key factors in ANALYSIS.

PLATEAU (LIU 陸): a type of GROUND without defects; an analogy for any equal, solid, and certain SITUATION; the best place for competition; one of the four types of GROUND.

RESOURCES, *provisions* (LIANG 糧): necessary supplies, most commonly food; one of the five targets of fire attacks.

RESTRAINT: see TIMING.

REWARD, *treasure, money* (BAO 賞): profit; wealth; the necessary compensation for competition; a necessary ingredient for

VICTORY; VICTORY must pay.

SCATTER, *dissipating* (SAN 散): to disperse; to lose UNITY; the pursuit of separate GOALS as opposed to a central MISSION; a situation that causes a FORCE to scatter; one of nine conditions or types of terrain.

SERIOUS, *heavy* (CHONG 重): any task requiring effort and skill; a SITUATION where resources are running low when you are deeply committed to a campaign or heavily invested in a project; a situation where opposition within an organization mounts; one of nine STAGES or types of TERRAIN.

SIEGE (GONG CHENG 攻城): to move against entrenched positions; any movement against an ENEMY'S STRENGTH; literally "strike city"; one of the four forms of attack; the least desirable form of attack.

SITUATION: see GROUND.

SPEED, *hurry* (SAI 馳): to MOVE over GROUND quickly; the ability to ADVANCE POSITIONS in a minimum of time; needed to take advantage of a window of opportunity.

SPREAD-OUT, *wide* (GUANG 廣): a surplus of DISTANCE; one of the six GROUND POSITIONS; opposite of CONSTRICTED.

SPY, *conduit, go-between* (GAAN 間): a source of information; a channel of communication; literally, an "opening between."

STAGE: see GROUND.

STANDARD, *proper, correct* (JANG 正): the expected behavior; the standard approach; proven methods; the opposite of SURPRISE; together with SURPRISE creates MOMENTUM.

STOREHOUSE, *house* (KU 庫): a place where resources are stockpiled; one of the five targets for fire attacks.

STORES, *accumulate, savings* (JI 糧): resources that have been stored; any type of inventory; one of the five targets of fire attacks.

STRENGTH, *fullness, satisfaction* (SAT 實): wealth or abundance or resources; the state of being crowded; the opposite of XU, empty.

SUPPLY WAGONS, *transport* (ZI 輜): the movement of RESOURCES through DISTANCE; one of the five targets of fire attacks.

SUPPORT, *supporting* (ZHII 支): to prop up; to enhance; a GROUND POSITION that you cannot leave without losing STRENGTH; one of six field positions; the opposite extreme of ENTANGLING.

SURPRISE, *unusual, strange* (QI 奇): the unexpected; the innovative; the opposite of STANDARD; together with STANDARDS creates MOMENTUM.

SURROUND: see CONFINED.

SURVIVE, *live, birth* (SHAANG 生): the state of being created, started, or beginning; the state of living or surviving; a temporary condition of fullness; one of five types of spies; the opposite of DEATH.

SYSTEM, *method* (FA 法): a set of procedures; a group of techniques; steps to accomplish a GOAL; one of the five key factors in analysis; the realm of groups who must follow procedures; the opposite of the LEADER.

TERRITORY, *terrain:* see GROUND.

TIMING, *restraint* (JIE 節): to withhold action until the proper time; to release tension; a companion concept to MOMENTUM.

TROOPS: see GROUPS.

UNITY, *whole, oneness* (YI 一): the characteristic of a GROUP that shares a PHILOSOPHY; the lowest number; a GROUP that acts as a unit; the opposite of DIVIDED.

UNOBSTRUCTED, *expert* (TONG 通): without obstacles or barriers; GROUND that allows easy movement; open to new ideas; one of six field positions; opposite of OBSTRUCTED.

VICTORY, *win, winning* (SING 勝): success in an endeavor; getting a reward; serving your mission; an event that produces more than it consumes; to make a profit.

WAR, *competition, army* (BING 兵): a dynamic situation in which POSITIONS can be won or lost; a contest in which a REWARD can be won; the conditions under which the rules of strategy work.

WATER, *river* (SHUI 水): a fast-changing GROUND; fluid CONDITIONS; one of four types of GROUND; an analogy for change.

WEAKNESS, *emptiness, need* (XU 虛): the absence of people or resources; devoid of FORCE; the point of ATTACK for an ADVANTAGE; a characteristic of GROUND that enables SPEED; poor; the opposite of STRENGTH.

WIN, *winning:* see VICTORY.

WIND, *fashion, custom* (FENG 風): the pressure of environmental forces.

Index of Topics in *The Art of War*

This index identifies significant topics, keyed to the chapters, block numbers (big numbers in text), and line numbers (tiny numbers). The format is chapter:block.lines.

About the Author

Gary Gagliardi

This book's award-winning translator and primary author, Gary Gagliardi, is America's leading authority on Sun Tzu's *The Art of War*. A frequent guest on radio and television talk shows, Gary has written over wenty books on strategy. Ten of his books on Sun Tzu's methods have won award recognition in business, self-help, career, sports, philosophy, multicultural, and youth nonfiction categories.

Gary began studying Sun Tzu's philosophy over thirty years ago. His understanding of strategy was proven in the business world, where his software company became one of the Inc. 500 fastest-growing companies in America and won numerous business awards. After selling his software company, Gary began writing about and teaching Sun Tzu's strategic philosophy full time.

He has spoken all over the world on a variety of topics concerning competition, from modern technology to ancient history. His books have been translated into many languages, including Japanese, Thai, Korean, Russian, Indonesian, and Spanish.

Today he splits his time between Seattle and Las Vegas, living with his wife, Rebecca, and travels extensively for speaking engagements all over the world.

garyg@suntzus.com

@strategygary

Want to learn more about Sun Tzu's strategy?

SunTzuS.com
SCIENCE OF STRATEGY INSTITUTE

eBooks
Audio books
Audio seminars
Online training

Art of War and Strategy Books By Gary Gagliardi

Sun Tzu's Art of War Rule Book in Nine Volumes

Sun Tzu's The Art of War Plus The Art of Sales: Strategy for the Sales Warrior

9 Formulas for Business Success: the Science of Strategy

The Golden Key to Strategy: Everyday Strategy for Everyone

The Art of War Plus The Chinese Revealed

The Art of War Plus The Art of Management: Straegy for Management Warriors

Art of War for Warrior Marketing: Strategy for Conquering Markets

The Art of War Plus The Art of Politics: Strategy for Campaigns (with Shawn Frost)

Making Money By Speaking: The Spokesperson Strategy

The Warrior Class: 306 Lessons in Strategy

The Art of War for the Business Warrior: Strategy for Entrepreneurs

The Art of War Plus The Warrior's Apprentice: Strategy for Teens

The Art of War Plus Strategy for Sales Managers: Strategy for Sales Groups

The Ancient Bing-fa: Martial Arts Strategy

Strategy Against Terror: Ancient Wisdom for Today's War

The Art of War Plus The Art of Career Building: Strategy for Promotion

Sun Tzu's Art of War Plus Parenting Teens

The Art of War Plus Its Amazing Secrets: The Keys to Ancient Chinese Science

Art of War Plus Art of Love: Strategy for Romance

www.ingramcontent.com/pod-product-compliance
Lightning Source LLC
Chambersburg PA
CBHW070505200326
41519CB00013B/2722